Society and Spirit

Society and Spirit

A Trinitarian Cosmology

Joseph A. Bracken, S. J.
With a Foreword by John B. Cobb, Jr.

Selinsgrove: Susquehanna University Press
London and Toronto: Associated University Presses

Associated University Presses
440 Forsgate Drive
Cranbury, NJ 08512

Associated University Presses
25 Sicilian Avenue
London WC1A 2QH, England

Associated University Presses
P.O. Box 39, Clarkson Pstl. Stn.
Mississauga, Ontario,
L5J 3X9 Canada

The paper used in this publication meets the requirements
of the American National Standard for Permanence of Paper
for Printed Library Materials Z39.48-1984.

Bracken, Joseph A.
   Society and spirit : a trinitarian cosmology / Joseph A. Bracken.
      p.   cm.
   Includes bibliographical references and index.
   ISBN 0-945636-21-0 (alk. paper)
   1. Cosmology.   2. Trinity.   3. Process theology.   4. Process
philosophy.   I. Title.
BT695.B68   1991
113—dc20   90-50601
                                                                 CIP

PRINTED IN THE UNITED STATES OF AMERICA

Contents

To My Jesuit Brothers
In Gratitude for over Forty Years of Life Together
This Book Is Affectionately Dedicated

Foreword

JOHN B. COBB, JR.

Joseph Bracken calls attention to the renewal of cosmology in our time. This trend runs superficially in quite the opposite direction from the dominant analytic, antifoundationalist, and deconstructive mood. But more closely viewed, Bracken shows that the emerging cosmology is more compatible with these interests than is widely supposed.

A central issue for any cosmological reconstruction is that of causality. It was Hume's and Kant's deconstruction of natural causality that brought an end to cosmology in the mainstream of modern philosophy. It has been Whitehead, above all, who has created a new way of understanding causality that makes possible new cosmological thinking.

Bracken places himself within this stream of renewed reflection and engages Whitehead and his followers in critical discussion about our way of understanding causality. On many points he accepts Whitehead's view. But at one point he believes that Whitehead did not go far enough, and he is particularly critical of "orthodox" interpreters, among whom he includes me.

We have so emphasized that individual actual entities are the causal agents, that the causal role of the ordinary objects of experience, or even of scientifically posited entities such as molecules and cells and fields, is obscure or misrepresented. Bracken acknowledges that Whitehead himself may be partly responsible for this one-sided interpretation, but he points out that Whitehead also offers a rich account of societies that has not been appreciated in the dominant secondary literature.

Bracken is correct in this critique. There has been and continues to be a great deal of distortion on just this point. It has led to revisionist developments from Whitehead that, in my view, have involved still more serious distortions. Bracken believes that by appreciating and developing Whitehead's discussion of societies, he can retain the central insights and contributions of Whitehead while overcoming a major limitation in the dominant

9

interpretation. Whether he has fully succeeded is open to question, but it is not open to question that he is rightly calling for a fuller discussion of a central feature of Whitehead's thought as well as proposing fruitful ways to develop cosmology today. We are in his debt.

A number of us Whiteheadians have understood the question about the causal efficacy of societies to be whether a society exercises any causal efficacy over and above that of its constituent members. These members are the "actual occasions" that are, for Whitehead, the final real things. For example, is there an efficacy of a living cell that cannot be attributed to the many actual occasions that jointly constitute the cell at any given moment? If so, there seems to be a unitary cellular occasion in addition to the molecular, atomic, and other constituents. But in the case of a rock, we have supposed, there is no such unitary functioning, so that the causal efficacy of the rock can be derived from that of its constituent molecular, atomic, and subatomic occasions. Our tendency has then been to neglect the effect on the causality of the constituent occasions of their shared role in constituting the rock. Sometimes we have written as if either a society includes a unifying actual entity among its members or it is a mere aggregate of its constituents. The result is that in discussing causal efficacy, what Whitehead calls social order has been neglected.

No thoughtful reader of Bracken's book can fall back into this way of posing the question. A society is certainly not an aggregate, and its causal efficacy is not of the sort that a mere aggregate can have. The actual occasions making up a society are what they are by virtue of being members of that society. Thus they are just as much constituted by the society as the society is constituted by them. The causality of the members cannot be abstracted from their participation in the society. Hence, even if the causal efficacy of the society is the collective causal efficacy of its members, the causal efficacy of its members is a function of this membership in the society. This is straight Whitehead, and many of Bracken's formulations give fine expression to a too-often-neglected point.

Whitehead goes beyond this in his doctrine of transmutation. Societies in their function as data for new occasions often constitute felt unities. They are physically felt as unities and these unities are physically transmitted to future occasions. This surely justifies speaking of the causal efficacy of societies.

All of this is to say that Bracken has made a major contribution to cosmology in general and to Whiteheadian cosmology in particular. To show this in more detail would require spelling out the views of a variety of major thinkers and showing how he resolves problems better than they. This would require more than is appropriate in a foreword; so I forbear. But for this contribution to the advance of the discussion we are in his debt.

That does not mean, of course, that I can follow him in all of his formulations. Some of these seem to subordinate the agency of individual occasions to the agency of societies in ways that do not follow from the central point, and some of the theological conclusions as well seem to be dependent on this subordination. But even where I cannot follow Bracken, I find him interesting. Whitehead said that it is more important that a proposition be interesting than that it be true. It is interesting propositions that evoke or provoke fresh thinking. Bracken's speculations certainly serve this function.

Bracken's most important theological conclusions deal with the Trinity. Bracken uses his development of Whitehead's doctrine of social order to overcome the dichotomy between Trinitarian doctrines that present the three as distinct beings and those that treat the three as simply three aspects of one being. He shows that his doctrine of the unity of societies, his proper emphasis that each member is what it is only by its inclusion of the others provides an alternative that well expresses much of what the traditional creeds have sought to say.

Bracken sees that process theologians in general have neglected this potential contribution of Whitehead's thought. We have followed the Western tradition in its emphasis on the oneness of God. Those of us who have concerned ourselves with the Trinitarian doctrine have sought the threeness in the distinguishable natures of God or in the complex pattern of God's ways of being both transcendent of, and immanent in, the world.

In the wider theological discussion, Juergen Moltmann is among those who have renewed within the Western context the primacy of the three as starting point for Trinitarian reflection. Bracken's cosmological speculations provide a basis for much of what Moltmann has done on this doctrine. Hence Bracken's work makes contact with important dimensions of the contemporary theological discussion and offers a path of advance within it.

One main reason for this move is to introduce relational existence fully into the internal life of God. Bracken certainly does this. Other process theologians believe that in the case of Whitehead's doctrine, the unity of God is so constituted by the divine

relations to all actuality and to all possibility, that the pluraliza-
tion of God as God is a theologically unneeded complexification.
Few of us are likely to be persuaded by Bracken's charge that
Whitehead's thought is implicitly pantheistic. Hence his claim
that Trinitarian doctrine is needed to avoid this outcome is un-
convincing. Still, this debate is theologically important, and
thanks to Bracken it will come alive within the community of
process theologians. At the same time, Bracken's work will introduce a quite new process voice in the wider Trinitarian debate.

   There are many reasons that Catholics should take the lead in
cosmological theology. Without cosmology theology cannot be
truly catholic in a general sense. Many Protestants have simply
accepted this limitation and allowed theology to be defined as
biblical hermeneutics. It is my hope that Catholics will resist this
narrowing of Christian thought. Those who do so have much to
gain from wrestling with the work of the greatest cosmologist of
this century, Alfred North Whitehead. That Bracken not only is
engaged in this wrestling, but that in the process he has developed original cosmological ideas is not only an important
contribution in itself but also a healthy invitation to others. May
many respond!

Preface

Ever since human beings first began to reflect about, and to discuss, their situation within the world of natural things, their most comprehensive ambition has been to talk sense about *the Universe as a whole*. In practical terms, this ambition has reflected the need to recognize where we stand in the world into which we have been born, to grasp our place in the scheme of things and to feel at home within it. In intellectual terms, meanwhile, it has stretched our powers of speculation and imagination like no other ambition, requiring us to extend the scope of our thoughts and our language beyond all natural boundaries, so that they become "all inclusive."[1]

With these words from the introduction to his recent book, *The Return to Cosmology*, Stephen Toulmin makes clear both the challenge and the risks inherent in the task of philosophical cosmology. He himself admits that some years ago he was quite skeptical of the enduring value of any such speculative schemes. But, as time passed and, in his judgment, as the scientific community itself began to think in more interdisciplinary and holistic terms, he felt the rekindling of a youthful interest in cosmological questions. Finally, in the lectures delivered in 1979 at Southern Methodist University and at the University of Chicago, which make up the third and last part of the above-named book, he makes a strong appeal for scientists, philosophers, and theologians to work together at a comprehensive new worldview. As he notes elsewhere in the book, "through most of its three-hundred-year history science has been associated far more closely with theology than with technology."[2] Hence, the time is ripe for scientists to take up again the underlying philosophical and theological questions associated with their research. Otherwise, they may gradually lose touch with their own humanity, the bonding with other human beings in terms of commonly accepted goals and values.

Encouraged by these words from one of the more distinguished philosopher-scientists of the present generation, I intend to set forth here at least a preliminary sketch of a new philosophical cosmology. As will be evident from the introduction onward, I am heavily influenced in this undertaking by the thought of Alfred North Whitehead. His magnum opus, *Process and Reality*, was, after all, subtitled *An Essay in Cosmology*.[3] At the same time, it will be clear that I am extending Whitehead's philosophy in a new direction, one, I trust, that is basically compatible with the thrust of his own reflections, but yet not one that he himself apparently envisioned.

That direction is implicitly given in the title of this book, namely, *Society and Spirit*. For I intend to develop further the Whiteheadian notion of a society as a preconstituted "environment" or patterned field of activity for the emergence of successive generations of "actual occasions." Thus understood, a Whiteheadian society is, in my judgment, a functioning ontological totality with a unified collective agency derived from the interrelated individual agencies of its constituent actual occasions from moment to moment. All of this will be explained at length in chapter 1. Here I only wish to emphasize that this represents an extension of Whitehead's thought in a direction that neither he himself nor any of his commentators thus far seems to have foreseen. Accordingly, one major reason for writing this book is to impress upon other Whiteheadians the need to do further thinking on this matter of the nature and activity of societies.

With reference to the second term in the title, namely, *spirit*, I also intend to develop Whitehead's thought in a new direction. In an article for *Process Studies* some years ago, the German philosopher-theologian Wolfhart Pannenberg complained that Whiteheadians have made little or no effort to link the master's thought with the mainstream of modern European philosophy.[4] By developing the notion of spirit in a Whiteheadian context, I hope to remedy that lacuna somewhat. For, in the second major division of the book, I will probe the affinities between Whitehead's thought and that of two great German Idealists, namely, Schelling and Hegel, who were themselves in every sense of the word cosmologists. Admittedly Whitehead was probably less interested in strictly teleological questions about the end of world history than either Schelling and Hegel.[5] But the reflections of Schelling on the nature of human subjectivity illuminate Whitehead's notion of an actual occasion as a self-constituting subject of experience; likewise, Hegel's development of the notion of objective spirit casts light on Whitehead's use of the category of society to describe civil society and the state. Hence, there is much to be learned from a judicious comparison of Whitehead's thought with that of Schelling and Hegel, even granted their obvious differences of perspective in the matter of a goal for human history.

The third and last part of the book will have to do with my own synthesis of the notions of society and spirit as set forth in parts one and two into a new understanding of the God-world relationship. The focus of my reflections here will be on the issue of panentheism, that is, the notion that human beings and indeed all finite creatures exist both in themselves and in God at the same time.[6] This has been a particularly difficult concept for process-oriented thinkers properly to articulate even though it is in many respects foundational for the entire enterprise of process philosophy and theology. For thus linking God and creatures in an ongoing dynamic relationship, one tends either to identify God with the world or the world with God. In the first case, one ends up with pancosmism; "God" is the name for the transcendent dimension of the world process as a cosmic whole. As Nancy Frankenberry points out, this seems to have been the thrust of Bernard Meland and Bernard Loomer in their efforts to work out a more "empirical" approach to the God-world relationship from a process-oriented perspective.[7] On the other hand, Whitehead himself, Charles Hartshorne, and many others who follow their lead seem to have unconsciously moved in the direction of pantheism. For while they clearly affirm the ontological independence of the world from God, nevertheless, the finite components of the world are perpetually perishing,[8] so that in the end God is the sole entity (or, for Hartshorne, the only set of actual occasions) that survives.

My own approach will be to suggest that only a trinitarian understanding of God as a community of three divine persons who share a common field of activity with all their creatures allows for a genuinely panentheistic understanding of the God-world relationship. For, as I shall make clear in chapters 6 and 7, only thus do God and creatures exist in ontological independence of one another and yet co-constitute a cosmic society that is in the final analysis Ultimate Reality. The fruit of my reflections on the key concepts of society and spirit in this book will be, then, a new cosmology, a new understanding of the God-world relationship within the overall parameters of a process-relational approach to reality. In this way, I will be doing what I can to meet Stephen Toulmin's challenge to fashion a new worldview appropriate for contemporary sensibilities.

JOSEPH A. BRACKEN, S. J.—

Acknowledgments

I would like to express my thanks to those who read individual chapters of this book in draft form and made helpful comments: chapter 1, John Cobb, School of Theology in Claremont, California; chapter 2, Abner Shimony, Boston University, and Henry Stapp, Lawrence Laboratories, University of California at Berkeley; chapter 3, Joseph Earley, Georgetown University, Washington, D.C.; chapter 4, Wolfhart Pannenberg, University of Munich, West Germany; chapter 5, George Lucas, Clemson University in South Carolina; chapters 6 and 7, Marjorie Suchocki, likewise of the School of Theology in Claremont. Naturally, the views set forth here are mine, not those of the individuals just cited. But these colleagues deserve credit for helping me in various ways to clarify my own position in each chapter.

Likewise, I here offer my thanks to the Macmillan Company for permission to quote extensively from the revised edition of *Process and Reality* by Alfred North Whitehead. I am also grateful to the editors of *International Philosophical Quarterly* and *Theological Studies* for permission to use in a revised and expanded form articles originally published in their journals: "Substance-Society-Natural System: A Creative Rethinking of Whitehead's Cosmology," *International Philosophical Quarterly* 25(1985): 3–13; "The Two Process Theologies: A Reappraisal," *Theological Studies* 46 (1985): 115–28. Finally, I would like to thank in a more general way all those who in a variety of forms gave me the support and encouragement that I needed to bring this task to completion.

Society and Spirit

Introduction: Being—Object of Thought or Subject of Experience?

Martin Heidegger is frequently cited as one of the most influential philosophers of the twentieth century. Above all in his penetrating critique of the Western metaphysical tradition, he raised questions about the reality of Being and the limits of human knowledge that in modified form continue to agitate the best philosophical minds of the present generation. Individuals as diverse in their thinking as Richard Rorty here in the United States and Jacques Derrida in Europe owe to Heidegger much of the impetus for their own critical reflection on the role of philosophy within academe, indeed, within the whole of Western culture.[1] Yet the legacy of Heidegger to contemporary philosophy is not without ambiguity. In particular, his vacillation on the function of subjectivity within human existence (*Dasein*) leaves many readers puzzled with respect to the proper starting-point for philosophical reflection.

For, on the one hand, subjectivity understood as the ontological correlate to objectivity, that is, as the capacity to represent objects to oneself, would seem to be an unfortunate inheritance from the philosophy of Descartes and other modern philosophers. The human subject in his or her preoccupation with the representations (*Vorstellungen*) of things thus never penetrates to the nonrepresentational Presence or Beingness of those same entities. She or he is even forgetful of the Beingness of her or his own existence, thereby reducing the self to one of its own representations.[2] On the other hand, as Paul Ricoeur points out, Heidegger kept returning throughout his career to the key relationship between *Sein* and *Dasein*, Being and human existence. Within this context, subjectivity or, as Heidegger terms it, *subjectity* resurfaces as the only access to the deeper meaning of Being available to humans.[3] Accordingly, even if one seeks the meaning of Being in the language of poets and in great works of art, as Heidegger recommends, the ultimate issue is still the nature of one's response to Being in and through these symbols, hence, reductively, a matter of subjectivity.

In this introduction I will set forth an overview of the history of Western philosophy that to some extent parallels Heidegger's celebrated critique of that same history but that in other respects represents an independent viewpoint, as my comments on Heidegger's own thought in the second part of the introduction should make clear. My conclusions in this overview may be summarized in advance as follows. In ancient and medieval philosophy, Being was first and foremost an object of thought in that God as the Supreme Being and First Cause of all other beings cannot be perceived by the senses but must be conceived through a process of reflection. With Descartes and the advent of modern philosophy, attention shifted to the human subject and his or her experiential "world" of representations, with the result that Being-questions were either ignored altogether or answered in terms of what it means to be human. Finally, in the postmodern period an antimetaphysical reaction has become established even among professional philosophers so that there is no longer any dominant worldview shared by reflective individuals. Hence, the stage seems to be set for the emergence of a new cosmology grounded in the processive and intersubjective character, not simply of human existence but of Being as such. A metaphysics of Becoming, in other words, is needed to replace the older metaphysics of Being, if only to provide a set of common presuppositions for different schools of thought to continue productive dialogue with one another.

An Overview of Western Philosophy

In making this brief survey, the generalizations thus set forth will inevitably be too broad to "prove" in any realistic sense of the term. But, taken together, they should make quite evident my own understanding of this history and of Heidegger's place within it. Keeping this in mind, my initial contention, as noted above, is that in ancient and medieval philosophy the meaning of Being was so intertwined with the activity of thinking that the one subtly came to be defined in terms of the other. That is, for an entity to exist was to be (at least) an object of thought; what could not be conceived did not exist, even as a possible existent. This is not to say, of course, that for individuals in ancient and medieval times only objects of thought existed. Clearly there had to be a distinction between actual and possible entities; some beings exist only in the mind whereas others exist both in the mind and in extramental reality. Likewise, some entities have minds to entertain objects of thought (including their own being as objects of self-awareness). Other entities either lack mind altogether so that they can serve only as objects of thought for entities with minds, or, in any case, lack self-awareness so that they cannot make their own being an object of thought. By implication, then, the higher one ascends on the "ladder" of Being, the more one becomes self-aware, able to make one's own being and activity an object of thought.

A cursory look at the philosophies of Plato, Aristotle, and Thomas Aquinas seems to confirm these observations. For Plato the Forms or Ideas constitute the world of Reality; physical things and their various "shadows" or imitations inhabit the world of Appearances.[4] While there is a hierarchy of Forms culminating in the Idea of the Good, all the Forms without exception are objects of thought; they cannot be perceived by the senses.[5] Thus Being for Plato is preeminently that which is (or at least can be) an object of thought. Whether the Idea of the Good is not only the supreme object of thought but likewise a Mind or thinking being is difficult to decide. For, as Frederick Copleston notes, it is then not clear what is the appropriate relationship between such a divine Mind and the Demiurge or World-Soul of the *Timaeus*.[6] At least in this respect, Aristotle's thinking is much more precise. He expressly identifies God or the Supreme Being in his philosophy with Mind, thought thinking itself.[7] Furthermore, God is the Prime Mover for the unending motion of the outermost celestial sphere and everything within it insofar as God is the supreme object of thought. As Aristotle comments: "The primary objects of desire and of thought are the same. For the apparent good is the object of appetite, and the real good is the primary object of rational wish."[8] Hence God is the Prime Mover insofar as the divine Being, thought thinking itself or eternal self-consciousness, is the object of rational wish for the "intelligence" governing the outermost celestial sphere and indeed for all other intelligent beings in the universe.

Here one might object that for Aristotle the first category of Being is not thought or the object of thought but rather substance.[9] Furthermore, a substance is able to be an object of thought because it already exists, not vice versa. Yet upon reflection one realizes that what is common to all substances, material and immaterial alike, is form, that by reason of which the substance is what it is. Form, however, for Aristotle as for Plato is the object of thought; as such, it cannot be perceived by the senses. Accordingly, even though Aristotle was fully aware that a given horse, for example, is not simply an instance of the species *horse* (as Plato apparently believed) but likewise an individualized concrete existent (this horse rather than that horse), he still dealt with it primarily as an object of thought, that is, in terms of its intelligible form, which can only be grasped in thought.[10] Aristotle, in other words, although far more empirically oriented than Plato, subconsciously was still an idealist. That is, he conceived the world as a hierarchically ordered scheme of objects of thought: from God as the supreme object of thought to prime matter as that which possessing no form of its own cannot be an object of thought, hence, is completely unintelligible in and of itself. God as the supreme object of thought, moreover, is the supreme existent. Prime matter, on the other hand, is reduced to a principle of being, that which can exist only in conjunction with form, the proper object of thought.

By common consent, the theology of Thomas Aquinas is a highly creative synthesis of reason and revelation, that is, Greek philosophy and the data of the Hebrew and Christian Bible. Since his chief task was the merger of these two disparate streams of thought, he inevitably could not be sharply critical of the theoretical presuppositions of Greek thought. Accordingly, the philosophical underpinning of his theology has the same idealistic orientation as the philosophies of Plato and Aristotle. That is, likewise for Aquinas, Being is implicitly defined in terms of thinking and the objects of thought. He begins his *Summa Theologiae*, for example, with rational proofs for the existence of God derived from application of the Aristotelian causes to the God-world relationship.[11] Within his scheme, therefore, God is the first principle of a metaphysical system in which the real existence of the world is taken for granted and its intelligibility in terms of material, formal, efficient and final causality is carefully worked out. Just as with Aristotle therefore, attention is given to the individual existent, not in terms of its concrete particularity, but with respect to its universal form or immaterial essence whereby it fits into a causal explanation of the universe. Even God is less an individual entity than a logical function within an a priori cosmological scheme.

Naturally, one could here object that in these early "Questions" of the *Summa Theologiae* Aquinas was merely setting forth what can be known about God through the use of natural reason before taking up the revealed knowledge of God as triune in Questions 29–43. In Question 44, however, where Aquinas begins his explanation of God as Creator, he does not work with the notion of God as triune but rather with the understanding of God as transcendent First Cause derived from the proofs for the existence of God in the opening questions. Hence, his model for the God-world relationship is not the triune God of Christian revelation, but the one God of natural reason. Furthermore, even within his exposition of the Trinity, he presupposes that God is one being and explains how God can likewise be three persons. That is, he explains how God through the immanent operations of knowing and loving the divine being or nature perfectly is, in fact, three persons, not one person. Philosophically speaking, therefore, Aquinas is still working with a notion of God much akin to that of Aristotle. That is, God is absolute or self-sufficient Being because the immanent operations of knowing and loving terminate in God's own nature or essence. God is, in other words, infinite Mind knowing and loving itself and as such the object of rational desire for all other entities whose being and activity are not self-contained.

Impressive as it is in other respects, Aquinas's metaphysics of the God-world relationship, accordingly, must be regarded as an a priori scheme that looks only to the universalizable dimensions of the entities in question, God included. As such, the metaphysical worldview of Aquinas (like that of Aristotle before him) consists in a hierarchically ordered set of concepts that are logically related to one another but only indirectly grounded in the lived experience of Aquinas and his followers. Its starting point, in other words, is not in the human being's perception of himself or herself as a concrete individual existent but in a reflection on that same concrete individual existent as a particular verification of universal metaphysical principles.[12]

Keeping this in mind, one sees immediately how René Descartes, the first philosopher of the modern period of Western philosophy, dramatically changed the rules of the game, so to speak. He began his philosophy, namely, with conscious reference to himself as a concrete individual subject of experience. Admittedly, his long-range intention was to set up a conceptual scheme with the same level of metaphysical generality as that of Aquinas and the other medieval scholastics. But, in describing at length his personal search for an absolutely certain starting point for philosophical reflection and, above all, in concluding that it

could only lie in the implicit affirmation of his own existence
within the act of reflection itself,[13] Descartes directed attention to
the reality of human subjectivity in a way that would have been
impossible within the more objective conceptual scheme of Aquinas and the other scholastics. Moreover, the subsequent history of Western philosophy has until recently tended to move in
the same direction, that is, to explore the inner world of human
subjectivity as the hermeneutical key to the understanding of the
entire cosmos. Concrete human experience rather than abstract
logic has been the touchstone for the validity of metaphysical
constructs.

Among early post-Cartesian philosophers, for example, John
Locke stands out as one who advocated the study of the process
of human knowing as the necessary precondition for trustworthy
knowledge of the external world. Furthermore, his "historical,
plain method" is an appeal, not to logic, but to common-sense
empirical observation of one's own conscious operations in dealing with the external world.[14] Ironically, this attempt to sidestep
the a priori approach of the medieval scholastic systems was
severely handicapped by Locke's uncritical acceptance of two a
priori assumptions out of Descartes's philosophy. First of all, he
accepted the Cartesian presupposition that the proper object of
human understanding is an idea or mental representation rather
than the extramental existent to which the idea as a sign refers.
Secondly, he accepted without reservation Descartes's analytical
approach to the study of ideas: namely, that the "building blocks"
of human knowledge are simple ideas derived from sensation or
immediate reflection upon sense data, and that complex ideas,
such as those of substance, cause and effect, are derived solely
from the activity of the mind in combining, comparing, and
separating simple ideas.[15] In this way, Locke could not logically
account for the objectivity of broader and more comprehensive
patterns of intelligibility within human experience. Thus he inadvertently paved the way for his successors in the tradition of
British empiricism.

Despite these pardonable errors in methodology and first principles, Locke and his successors were breaking new ground in
the study of human subjectivity as the implicit basis for knowledge of the external world. Furthermore, while many philosophers on the continent were still preoccupied with the
traditional metaphysical questions of the schoolmen, Immanuel
Kant recognized the importance of the empiricist tradition in
England and devised his own "critical" philosophy as a con-

scious response to the skepticism about the possibility of scientific knowledge resulting therefrom (particularly from the writings of David Hume).[16] In retrospect, one sees that Kant's vindication of *synthetic a priori* judgments as the metaphysical basis for scientific knowledge of the world is far less significant than his overall project of exploring the ordering and synthesizing activities of the human mind. Furthermore, Kant's successors, the German Idealists, introduced a new cosmological perspective into the study of human subjectivity, which they themselves and their contemporaries only grasped in fragmentary fashion.

Fichte, for example, in the first introduction to his *Wissenschaftslehre* made clear that what human beings perceive as objects of experience are not things in themselves with an independent ontological reality but rather products of the synthesizing activity of the preconscious transcendental ego.[17] While one might indeed question whether the full reality of the object of experience can be thus accounted for through the synthesizing activity of human intelligence, nevertheless his deeper insight remains valid that the mind as such is pure activity and that its nature as pure activity can only be grasped reflexively in intuiting the primordial unity of subject and object within human consciousness. Thus, in grasping the unity in difference between the "I" as thinking and the "I" as thought, I intuit their suprasensible unity in terms of the activity of thought within my own consciousness. This insight into the nature of human subjectivity as primarily an activity *(ein Tun)* rather than as a preexistent agent *(ein Tätiges)* capable of activity,[18] provides a much more dynamic understanding of Being, what it means to be, than was possible in pre-Kantian metaphysics with its focus on relatively permanent things or substances. But the full force of this insight was lost in Fichte's *subjective* idealism, according to which the nonhuman world simply serves as a temporary check *(Anstoss)* or limit to the human ego in its restless striving for full self-realization.

Schelling, on the other hand, in his early *Naturphilosophie* ascribed to Nature or objective Being the same underlying reality, namely, pure activity, as Fichte prescribed for the transcendental ego. This means, as Schelling explains, that nothing in Nature is permanent. Everything is reproduced anew from moment to moment by the underlying activity of Nature so that only the appearance of permanence is given to the senses.[19] Furthermore, Nature as a whole must be represented as a continuously expanding system or organization of natural entities (*Naturprodukte*). Each of these natural entities is a balance of rival forces (*Aktionen*) within Nature itself: that is, forces of attraction and repulsion that achieve a momentary synthesis in the entity under consideration.[20] Thus Nature, understood as pure unending activity, is initially undifferentiated, but it spontaneously divides into opposing forces whose synthesis or reunification at various levels constitutes the world of natural entities.

This same thought-pattern whereby duality arises out of an antecedent undifferentiated unity and exists only to bring into being various forms of differentiated unity—what Hermann Zeltner calls *das dynamische Gleichgewichtsprinzip* within Schelling's philosophy[21]—reappears in a somewhat modified form in his philosophy of identity of the early 1800s and in the controversial *Of Human Freedom*, published in 1809. In the latter work, however, the rival principles are no longer associated with mind and various kinds of subject-object relationships, but with will and the operation of rational and nonrational principles within the divine mind, human consciousness, and subhuman creation.[22] This focus on the conflictual character of processes within Nature, human consciousness, and even the divine consciousness added considerable depth and originality to Schelling's earlier published works. But the very thought of a nonrational principle within human and, above all, divine consciousness was too great a stumbling block for most of Schelling's contemporaries, with the result that they did not recognize the revolutionary character of his reflections in *Of Human Freedom*.

In the meantime, moreover, Hegel's star had risen with the publication of the *Phenomenology of Mind* in 1807. The latter was both a masterpiece of rigorous logical thinking and an impressive synthesis of much of the scientific knowledge of the day. Hence, it together with his later works enjoyed great popularity because they seemed to represent a singular triumph of the human spirit, concrete proof that the human mind at a properly philosophical level of reflection is the mirror image of the divine mind at work in nature and human history.[23] Moreover, Hegel incorporated within his philosophy many of the themes earlier associated with Fichte and Schelling. His dynamic interpretation of the Concept (*Begriff*), for example, clearly reflects Fichte's understanding of the transcendental ego and Schelling's assumption that God or absolute reason is the identity of thought thinking itself. But, unlike the other two, Hegel did not merely postulate that the Concept is the creative ground within nature and history. He first established its rational nature or essence as a system of dialectically related logical concepts and then proved that nature and human history ultimately made sense only if interpreted in the light of that same system of categories. His philosophical system is thus aptly called *absolute* idealism since it aspires to total self-sufficiency, proof of its logical starting point in and through the system as a whole.[24]

With the speculative triumph of Hegel's philosophy, however, an antimetaphysical reaction arose, which to some extent has endured to this day. First of all, Karl Marx and his followers asserted the primacy of *praxis* over *theoria;* that is, critical reflection in the service of a revolutionary movement is ultimately more insightful than the attempt by a single individual simply to understand the status quo in terms of some abstract scheme.[25] Moreover, in their judgment, metaphysical thinking has quite often impeded needed social change since it covertly serves as a form of ideology to protect the interests of the ruling classes in society. Later in the nineteenth century, Friedrich Nietzsche proclaimed the death of God, thereby predicting in symbolic language the eventual downfall of the dominant God-centered pattern of philosophical reflection in the West. Then, at the beginning of the present century, Sigmund Freud uncovered the subconscious base of human consciousness, the conflicts of infrapersonal impulse and desire that systematically distort the deliverances of human rationality. The long-term effect of these reflections has been, by and large, to discredit altogether or at least seriously to question the possibility of achieving objective knowledge of the world through analysis of the a priori structures of human consciousness. These "masters of suspicion," as David Tracy calls them,[26] have permanently impaired the original naive trust of Westerners in self-consciousness, the power of the human mind to critique its own operations, and thus by degrees to achieve full rationality.[27]

The End of Philosophy?

It is in this context that the thought of Martin Heidegger, in particular his polemic against the subjectivism and the anthropocentrism of modern thought, has to be understood. Heidegger is the professional philosopher who notes with alarm that philosophers and other reflective thinkers no longer take seriously the question of Being. Looking back through the history of Western metaphysics, he notes, first of all, that for a number of reasons (religious and cultural as well as purely philosophical) ontology became onto-theology in the hands of early Christian thinkers. Being was identified with God as the Supreme Being and the elaborate system of causal relationships between God and creatures referred to above became the subject matter of metaphysics.[28] Yet this situation was in its own way preferable to that which prevailed in modern philosophy from Descartes onward. For the medieval thinkers were at least aware of the primacy of the question of Being, even if they unconsciously confused Being with God as the Supreme Being. Descartes and subsequent modern thinkers, while they rid themselves of the logical apparatus of medieval scholasticism through recourse to the experience of the individual human subject, gradually lost sight of the key question of the deeper reality of Being altogether. Heidegger's critique of the Western metaphysical tradition, therefore, is simultaneously directed at two quite different schools of thought. Against those who still adhere to classical metaphysics, he objects that they are locked into a priori interpretations of human experience in terms of Aristotelian causes; thus they miss the reality of Being as that which transcends cause-effect relationships. Against the tendency of modern secular thinkers to ground the value of philosophical reflection exclusively in its pragmatic usefulness for improving the quality of human life, he objects that they are no longer doing philosophy but at best philosophical anthropology. That is, they are studying human being in all its empirical dimensions; but they are not getting at the roots of human being in Being itself as a cosmic process of incomprehensible proportions.

Heidegger's own solution to this question of the deeper meaning of Being, however, is not very satisfactory. Above all, as represented by works published after the celebrated turn (Kehre) in his thinking from Dasein to Sein, he seems to adopt a meditative, idiosyncratic approach to the various self-manifestations of Being in human experience.[29] Gone, therefore, is the attempt at a rigorous analysis of human experience so characteristic of Being and Time; likewise gone is the intense effort of an Auseinandersetzung with the Western metaphysical tradition that molded his thought in Kant and the Problem of Metaphysics and other early works. Admittedly, in The End of Philosophy and other publications of his later period, he suggests that, while metaphysics is dead, philosophy itself will survive in an altered form. Joan Stambaugh comments:

The end of philosophy does not mean for Heidegger that philosophy as such has become a thing of the past, a pursuit which has outlived its meaningfulness for human nature. Nor does Heidegger mean that philosophy in its essential sense has fulfilled its telos, that the "hard labor of the concept" (Hegel) has accomplished its task. Rather, he means that philosophy as *metaphysics* has come to a completion which now offers the possibility of a more original way of thinking.[30]

But what is this more original way of thinking? Heidegger's own somewhat enigmatic way of thinking and writing in the later years of his life offers exasperatingly few clews to the reader.

Likewise, contemporary thinkers strongly influenced by Heidegger, such as Jacques Derrida and Richard Rorty, are much clearer in their critique of classical metaphysics than they are in proposals for the future of philosophical reflection. Rorty, for example, rejects the "ocular metaphor" for human knowledge, that is, knowing as "seeing" things as they really are.[31] For, in his judgment, this leads to foundationalism, an understanding of reality as grounded in unchanging concepts or principles grasped by the mind intuitively insofar as the latter is the mirror of nature. Yet his own proposal for philosophy as "edifying" rather than "systematic," that is, as an ongoing conversation rather than as an inquiry into the nature of things, is ultimately parasitical upon the various forms of systematic philosophy that it critiques. As he himself notes, edifying philosophy is essentially reactive against systematic philosophy; hence, it must remain "peripheral" to the "mainstream" of philosophical reflection that is necessarily systematic in character.[32] Furthermore, Rorty's own ideal of philosophy as conversation between equals in an atmosphere of mutual trust would benefit greatly from a prior understanding of truth as inherently processive and communitarian. Yet, to establish this last point, one would necessarily have to engage in systematic philosophy, that is, in some fashion describe how things are.

Derrida's critique of the Western metaphysical tradition focuses on its inevitable "logocentrism": "All the metaphysical determinations of truth, and even the one beyond metaphysical ontotheology that Heidegger reminds us of, are more or less immediately inseparable from the instance of the logos, or of a reason thought within the lineage of the logos, in whatever sense it is understood."[33] Logos, moreover, whether divine or human, at work in the cosmos at large or within the individual human being, has always been thought to express itself, first and fore-

most, in the spoken word and only secondarily in writing as the
defective complement of the spoken word. Derrida, however,
conjectures that writing, understood as a self-contained system
of signs that have no intrinsic meaning apart from their necessary
connection with one another, is a much more significant analogue or metaphor for the actual workings of the human mind than
the classical understanding of speech as the self-expression of an
enduring human or divine subject of experience.[34] On the other
hand, Derrida freely admits that the project of deconstruction
can only be exercised upon texts of a systematic or constructive
character, that is, upon texts that attempt to specify the way
things are. As he says in "Structure, Sign and Play in the Discourse of the Human Sciences": "There is no sense in doing
without the concepts of metaphysics in order to shake metaphysics. We have no language—no syntax and no lexicon—
which is foreign to this history; we can pronounce not a single
destructive proposition which has not already had to slip into
the form, the logic, and the implicit presuppositions of precisely
what it seeks to contest."[35] Thus, like Richard Rorty as noted
above, Derrida is inevitably dependent upon an ongoing history
of metaphysical reflection for the survival of his own approach to
philosophy. Furthermore, one might well ask whether the key
notion of différance—which Derrida describes as "the systematic
play of differences" between concepts and thus as "the possibility of conceptuality, of a conceptual process and system in
general"[36]—is not itself a metaphor for something else that altogether transcends the sphere of human language and culture:
that is, Being itself which ex hypothesi is not a being but is
instantiated in all the entities present in the universe and in their
systematic interrelatedness at any given moment. For, in that
case, Derrida might also profit from an exploration of the possibilities for further systematic philosophy latent within his own
antimetaphysical approach to philosophy.[37]

In any event, what seems clear from the present survey of
Western philosophical reflection is that neither classical metaphysics, with its focus on Being as a timeless object of thought,
nor modern post-Cartesian systems of thought, with their starting
point and terminus in the experience of the empirical human
subject, can provide the necessary framework for a new ontology,
a new answer to the deeper meaning and reality of Being. Classical metaphysics, to be sure, raises Being-questions but in a fixed
logical context that inhibits reflection on Being as a dynamic and
processive reality within human experience. Post-Cartesian phi-

losophies, on the other hand, focus on human experience but neglect the more fundamental issues of the meaning and reality of Being. What is needed, accordingly, is a mediating third position: that is, a new cosmology that raises the traditional Being-questions, but in a way that is grounded in the experience of the human subject.

Here the "reformed subjectivist principle" of Alfred North Whitehead bears close scrutiny. According to that principle, "apart from the experiences of subjects there is nothing, nothing, nothing, bare nothingness."[38] Whitehead does not refer here simply to human subjects, since that would be nothing more than a repristination of Fichte's subjective idealism. Rather, he is suggesting that whatever appears to exist as an objective reality in common sense experience (for example, tables, chairs, plants, animals, human beings, and their various forms of social organization) is, in point of fact, the effect or product of myriad sub-microscopic momentary subjects of experience in dynamic interrelation. Human beings have concrete experience of this universal subjectivity in that their own temporal consciousness is a "society" or series of such momentary submicroscopic subjects of experience in rapid succession.[39] But, Whitehead quickly adds, such immediate experience of universal subjectivity is only analogous to the subjectivity of the "actual occasions" (or "actual entities"), as he calls them, which make up a table, chair, plant, animal, even the body of a human being (apart from her or his mind).[40]

In effect, what Whitehead is proposing with his doctrine of actual occasions is not a picture of reality, a description of the way things really are, but an extended metaphor or what Ian Barbour calls a "theoretical model," that is, "a symbolic representation of aspects of the world which are not directly accessible to us."[41] As such, it represents a deliberate generalization of certain familiar "processes" or "mechanisms" within reality in order to construct a theory about the nature of reality as a whole. To be specific, in Whitehead's philosophy the experience of process or becoming within human temporal consciousness is carefully analyzed in terms of its logical antecedents and consequents so as to serve as a model for the reality of process within all other entities, finite and infinite alike. Yet, while such a model should be taken seriously, it should not be taken literally.[42] As Whitehead himself comments in the introductory chapter to *Process and Reality*, "Words and phrases must be stretched toward a generality foreign to their ordinary usage; and however such elements of language be stabilized as technicalities, they remain metaphors mutely appealing for an imaginative leap."[43]

Rorty's critique of classical metaphysics in terms of foundationalism, therefore, in my judgment does not apply to Whitehead's categoreal scheme since the latter is simply an imaginative scheme whose ongoing validity is dependent upon its applicability and adequacy to the facts of experience.[44] Some Whiteheadians, to be sure, might argue that Whitehead's scheme has been sufficiently verified in the light of concrete experience, so that it no longer should be considered simply a metaphor. But, if so, they are inadvertently guilty of what Whitehead himself terms "the fallacy of misplaced concreteness," namely, treating a conceptual scheme as if it were more real than the reality it is intended to describe.[45]

On the other hand, as I see it, Whitehead's philosophy is guilty of what Derrida calls logocentrism. That is, within Whitehead's categoreal scheme, God is clearly the center of the cosmic process. Admittedly, in *Process and Reality* he claims that "God and the world are the contrasted opposites in terms of which Creativity achieves its supreme task of transforming disjoined multiplicity, with its diversities in opposition, into concrescent unity, with its diversities in contrast."[46] But, since God is the only actual entity whose process of becoming never ends, God is, in effect, the principle of unity for the world process, that entity whose "consequent nature" sums up the entire past history of the universe.[47] I will have much more to say about this feature of Whitehead's philosophy in subsequent chapters, notably, in chapters 6 and 7. For the moment, I only wish to point out that my focus in this book on the supplementary metaphors of *society* and *spirit* is consciously intended to overcome the residual logocentrism in Whitehead's philosophy. For, strictly speaking, a Whiteheadian society has no center. In Whitehead's own words, it is a "nexus" of actual occasions, each of which reproduces as part of its internal self-constitution a "common element of form" or pattern of intelligibility, that is their binding principle.[48] Hence, every actual occasion is *a* center of the society in question, but none is *the* center. Thus, if, as I shall maintain in part three of this book, the ultimate reality is not God as an individual existent but a cosmic society in while all finite entities exist in dynamic interrelationship with the three divine persons of Christian theology, then, in principle, logocentrism is overcome.[49] Similarly, my employment of the notion of spirit is with conscious reference to what Hegel called "objective spirit," spirit insofar as it is shared by individual entities in dynamic interaction as members of a society or social network of some kind.

My intention in this book, of course, is not to offer a direct rebuttal to the arguments of either Richard Rorty or Jacques Derrida about the deficiencies of classical metaphysics. Rather, it is to set forth a metaphysical scheme that is self-consciously metaphorical (and thus, I trust, impervious to the charge of foundationalism leveled by Rorty at other systems of metaphysics). Likewise, insofar as it is consistently processive and communitarian in its understanding of the nature of reality, it may evade the pitfall of logocentrism, which Derrida thinks is endemic to all systems of metaphysics. The reader, however, will ultimately have to decide whether I am guilty of self-deception here. In any event, in the next three chapters, I will set forth my understanding of a Whiteheadian society (which differs in some measure from the orthodox Whiteheadian interpretation of it) and show its applicability to certain controversial issues in physics and chemistry. Then, in part two of the book, I will elaborate my understanding of spirit in heavy dependence upon the German Idealists, Schelling and Hegel. Finally, in the third and last part of the book, I will combine the two notions of society and spirit to sketch a new panentheistic understanding of the God-world relationship, one in which God and creatures cooperate to produce an ever-expanding cosmic society.

Part One
Society

1

Substance-Society-Natural System

Surely one of the more significant thinkers in the philosophy of nature at this time is Ivor Leclerc. First in *The Nature of Physical Existence* and more recently in *The Philosophy of Nature*, he has reviewed key concepts in the discipline (for example, matter and motion, space and time, extension) and come to the conclusion that they are outdated in view of contemporary developments in the natural sciences.[1] Consequently, in the latter half of each of these books, he sets forth his own revised understanding of these same concepts. For that purpose, he is by his own admission heavily indebted to I. Kant in his precritical period, G. W. Leibniz, and, above all, A. N. Whitehead, even though he himself espouses a modified Aristotelianism in these matters. While basically agreeing with his critique of the early modern (sixteenth- and seventeenth-century) understanding of the nature of physical existence, I find myself nevertheless contesting his proposal to repristinate the Aristotelian category of substance as the key concept within a new philosophy of nature. Instead, it seems to me that Whitehead's notion of society, suitably modified to adjust to Leclerc's incisive criticism of its use within Whitehead's philosophy, would be a more suitable paradigm to describe the functioning unities of common-sense experience. Furthermore, a Whiteheadian society, thus reinterpreted, seems to bear a striking resemblance to what Ervin Laszlo calls a "natural system" with the latter's wide-ranging applicability not only to organisms but likewise to suborganic entities such as atoms and molecules and to supraorganic realities such as human communities and environmental systems. Thus, as I see it, the notion of society includes what is normally meant by substance, but not vice versa. Hence, society rather than substance should be the foundational concept of a contemporary cosmology.

I will begin by summarizing those parts of Leclerc's work that are pertinent to my own hypothesis. In tracing the history of key concepts within the philosophy of nature, he shows that Leibniz's *Monadology*, though little understood by his own generation, was nevertheless a watershed within the discipline. For, the impasse between those who conceived matter as composed of indivisible atoms and those who understood matter in terms of extension, and therefore as infinitely divisible in principle, could only be resolved by moving the discussion on the nature of matter to a new frame of reference. That is, Leibniz proposed that the concepts of matter and extension do not pertain to individual entities as such but only to such entities in combination with one another.[2] Hence one can hold with the atomists that material reality is ultimately composed of indivisible entities. But, since these entities are themselves immaterial and only their relations with one another are extensive, then matter remains for the purposes of abstract thought infinitely divisible. Material bodies, in other words, de facto have a finite number of parts; but the extension proper to the body as a result of the structural relationship of the parts to one another can be mathematically divided up to infinity.

Even more important for a new philosophy of nature, however, is Leibniz's hypothesis that the terms body and substance are not interchangeable. Bodies are material realities; substances, that is, the ultimate physical existents, are immaterial entities. Material bodies are made up of immaterial substances in their dynamic relations with one another. Thus Leibniz agreed with Newton in the latter's contention that the character of the whole must be derived from the character of the constituent parts; but he disagreed with him in his other contention that the constituent parts must themselves have the character of the whole. The right combination of immaterial parts will produce a material whole of a certain character, but the parts themselves need not be material.[3] The material whole, then, is greater than (or, in any case, other than) an aggregate, simply the sum of its parts.

This last statement might lead one to conclude that Leibniz was consciously reintroducing Aristotelian metaphysical principles into the philosophy of nature at a time when material atomism, the doctrine that all macroscopic realities are in fact aggregates of inert bits of matter in purely extrinsic relationships to one another, was enjoying great popularity in European intellectual circles. This conclusion, moreover, is reinforced when one reflects carefully on Leibniz's doctrine of "monads," the immaterial substances that make up material bodies. For each of these monads, like an Aristotelian substance, contains its own entelechy or immanent principle of being and activity.[4] Yet, curiously enough, it is at the same time unlike an Aristotelian substance in that its principle of being and activity is purely immanent, affecting only the internal constitution of the monad itself. It has, in other words, no causal efficacy on other monads so as to constitute with them a material body as a subsistent reality in its own right. That is, material bodies are only apparent ontological unities; in fact, they are aggregates of monads, immaterial entities with a divinely ordained pre-established harmony with one another so as to give the appearance of a unitary reality.[5]

Here, of course, is where Leclerc parts company with Leibniz since the latter is clearly inconsistent in his repristination of Aristotelian principles on this point. Leibniz should have provided for the objective (as opposed to the merely subjective or phenomenal) interaction of the monads on one another, much as the material elements within an Aristotelian substance by their interaction co-constitute the new objective reality of the substance. The substantial form, then, is the intelligible pattern governing the de facto "actings" of the monads on one another at any given moment.[6] Leclerc is appealing here to a more dynamic understanding of substantial form within Aristotle's metaphysics than was perhaps customary in the past, but he would seem to be supported in this line of thought by other contemporary Aristotle commentators. Werner Marx and Ernst Tugendhat, for example, both agree that, for Aristotle, Being is activity and that the substantial form is the principle whereby Being as activity is particularized or individuated with respect to a given set of material elements.[7]

Leclerc freely admits that he is heavily indebted to Alfred North Whitehead both for his interpretation of Leibniz's *Monadology* and for the more dynamic understanding of Aristotle's substantial form. But, says Leclerc, there is a major difference between his own understanding of substance and the Whiteheadian notion of a "society," that is, a spatially and temporally organized group of "actual occasions." For, like Leibnizian monads, actual occasions for Whitehead are immaterial subjects of experience totally involved with their internal self-constitution and thus unable to exercise transeunt causality upon one another.[8] Hence, Whiteheadian societies are reductively only aggregates of actual occasions and not the equivalent of ontological actualities or organisms in the Aristotelian sense of the term. In this respect, Leclerc feels a closer affinity with the precritical

Kant, who likewise accepted Leibniz's hypothesis of immaterial monads as constitutive parts of material bodies, but (like Leclerc) insisted on the physical interaction of the monads on one another so as to bring into being the concrete material entity.[9]

My own comments on this matter would be twofold. On the one hand, Leclerc seems to have given a subjectivistic interpretation to Whitehead's doctrine of actual occasions, which many, if not most, Whiteheadians would find repugnant to the basic thrust of the latter's thought. That is, as already noted, Leclerc suggests that each actual occasion is active only with respect to its own self-constitution and thus in no way exercises transeunt causality upon other occasions. Yet Whitehead refers to actual occasions as "subject/superjects" precisely to accentuate their role in the self-constitution of the next generation of occasions. As he says in *Process and Reality*: "What is felt *subjectively* by the objectified actual entity is transmitted *objectively* to the concrescent actualities which supersede it. In [John] Locke's phraseology the objectified actual entity is then exerting 'power,'" that is, exercising transeunt causality upon those subsequent actual entities.[10] Even more pointedly, in a later work, *Adventures of Ideas,* he takes note of the "object-to-subject structure of experience" and describes it as "the doctrine of the immanence of the past energizing in the present."[11] Subsequent actual entities, to be sure, ultimately "decide" how to deal with this causal influence from the past; but they cannot simply ignore it since it forms the objective world out of which they must constitute their own being.[12] Hence, Leclerc would seem to have misread Whitehead on this key point.[13]

On the other hand, when one considers how underdeveloped the notion of society is in Whitehead's philosophy and how little attention has been given to that topic by Whiteheadians, it may well be that Leclerc is correct in his contention that Whitehead clearly wanted a society to be more than an aggregate but never set forth a strong enough case to support that claim.[14] Moreover, distinguished Whiteheadians like Charles Hartshorne and John Cobb seem to have addressed the problem, at best, only in part; that is, they have focused attention on one special kind of society, namely, the "structured" society that is constituted out of subsocieties and that includes as one of its subsocieties a "personally ordered" society that is dominant over all the others. Examples would be the human mind insofar as it is dominant over the subsocieties of actual occasions, first, in the brain and then in the entire body; likewise God, insofar as God is understood to be the "soul" of the universe, dominant over all the finite entities in existence at any given moment. Using this model of a personally ordered structured society, they then conclude that cells, molecules, and even atoms are "compound individuals," exercising agency in and through their "regnant" society of actual occasions.[15]

The key metaphysical issue here is that of agency. For in Whitehead's philosophy, "agency belongs exclusively to actual occasions."[16] Thus, given the fact that not only actual occasions, but also molecules and cells, appear to exercise agency, then Leclerc has reason to argue against Whitehead that they, too, are individual existents, albeit of a higher order than actual occasions; in effect, they are Aristotelian substances. Hartshorne and Cobb respond to Leclerc's critique of Whitehead's doctrine by urging that cells, molecules, and perhaps even atoms are personally ordered structured societies in which agency is exercised for the whole by the current occasion within the dominant subsociety. Thus Whitehead is vindicated since agency is still exercised solely by actual occasions even within these "compound individuals."

My own understanding of Whiteheadian societies would represent a compromise between these two positions. With Hartshorne and Cobb, I would argue that atoms and molecules are structured societies of actual occasions, not Aristotelian substances. Yet, with Leclerc I would contend that atoms and molecules do exercise agency. Their agency, however, is in each case not the agency of an individual existent, but rather the collective agency proper to a society, that is, the collation or fusion of all the individual agencies of constituent actual occasions. Furthermore, while a society thus exercises agency, it does not make decisions with respect to its ongoing self-constitution. Only actual occasions make such decisions; societies come into being and exercise collective agency in virtue of those individual decisions. Within some societies, to be sure, there is a dominant subsociety, the decisions of whose constituent occasions heavily influence the collective agency of the entire society. But, even here, the society behaves as it does because of the decisions of all its constituent occasions.[17] Finally, it should be noted that Leclerc also holds that the agency of a molecule or cell is a collective agency; for its agency "arises from the agency of the constituents, by each of the constituents contributing its agency to constitute an integral combined agency."[18] The difference between his understanding of collective agency and mine, of course, is that he regards it as ultimately the agency of a new individual existent, whereas I consider it as always a collective agency, the agency proper to a society acting in and through its constituent occasions.

To clarify my position, I will now show its basic coherence with Whitehead's own remarks on the nature of societies. In the chapter entitled "The Order of Nature" in *Process and Reality*, Whitehead notes, first of all, that "a society is more than a set of entities to which the same class-name applies: that is to say, it involves more than a merely mathematical conception of order. To constitute a society, the class-name has got to apply to each member by reason of genetic derivation from other members of that same society."[19] A few lines later, he adds, "Thus a set of entities is a society (i) in virtue of a 'defining characteristic' shared by its members, and (ii) in virtue of the presence of the defining characteristic being due to the environment provided by the society itself." Thus a society functions as an environment. In the next chapter, where I consider possible applications of Whitehead's philosophy in the area of contemporary physics, I will refer to it as a field. But whether it be termed an environment or a field, a society is not an oversized actual occasion or an aggregate of occasions. It is rather the necessary physical context for the ongoing emergence of actual occasions in dynamic inter-relation. As such, it has "some element of order in it, persisting by reason of the genetic relations between its own members."[20] It is, in other words, the bearer of the pattern or structural rela-tionship between occasions (and between successive generations of occasions) whereby they are (and continue to be) this rather than that higher-order entity (for example, an atom, molecule, cell, or entire organism).

Whitehead, accordingly, was quite consistent when he noted in *Process and Reality* that actual entities "are the final real things of which the world is made up."[21] For, a society is not itself a thing but that which comes into existence as a result of the dynamic interrelation of things, that is, actual entities (or actual occasions). Moreover, once constituted, it serves as the principle of continuity between successive generations of actual entities so that they continue to assume basically the same structural rela-tionships as in the past. "Thus in a society, the members can only exist by reason of the laws which dominate the society, and the laws only come into being by reason of the analogous characters of the members of the society."[22] Each new generation of actual occasions by their collective prehension of the pattern or structural relationship existing among their predecessors will both reproduce and in some subtle way slightly modify that same pattern for themselves, although only their own successors in the society will directly prehend what modifications they actually made. A society, then, "does not in any sense create the complex of eternal objects which constitutes its defining characteristic." This is the task of its constituent actual occasions from one generation to the next. "It only elicits that complex into importance for its members, and secures the reproduction of its membership."[23] In other words, as already noted, it acts as the principle of continuity between successive generations of occasions so that, as Whitehead comments in *Adventures of Ideas:* "The real actual things that endure are all societies. They are not actual occasions. . . . Thus a society, as a complete existence and as retaining the same metaphysical status, enjoys a history expressing its changing reactions to changing circumstances. But an actual occasion has no such history. It never changes. It only becomes and perishes."[24]

Granted that a society, without being an actual entity, is nevertheless an ontological reality (a nonactual entity, if you will), does it exercise agency? Here, in opposition to Hartshorne and Cobb, I would argue that it does exercise agency; but that, as noted above, its agency is a collective agency derivative from the individual agencies of its constituent actual occasions. It should be immediately added, of course, that among those constituent occasions might well be one that is clearly "regnant" over all the others (for example, the latest member in the personally ordered society of "living" actual occasions that constitutes the "soul" in an animal organism). But the individual agency that it therewith exercises is fused with the individual agencies of the other occasions (both animate and inanimate) so as to constitute the collective agency of the entire structured society. Hence, the structured society as a whole is the ontological agent even though it exercises that agency principally (though not exclusively) through one of its constituent actual occasions.

Whitehead seems to have much the same point in mind when he notes in *Process and Reality:* "There will be the 'subservient' nexūs and the 'regnant' nexūs within the same structured society. This structured society will provide the immediate environment which sustains each of its sub-societies, subservient and regnant alike."[25] A few lines later, he adds: "A complex inorganic system of interaction is built up for the protection of 'entirely living' nexūs, and the originative actions of the living elements are protective of the whole system. On the other hand, the reactions of the whole system provide the intimate environment required by the 'entirely living' nexūs." Whitehead, to be sure, is thinking here principally of nexuses of living actual occasions within plants and primitive animal organisms rather than of the "soul" in more complex animal species, which is organized as a personally ordered society. But the ontological principle of totality is operative in both cases; that is, the structured society exists and acts as a totality, a unitary whole, albeit in and through the diverse individual agencies of its constituent occasions.

Clarity on this key issue might be gained if we briefly review the agency required for the existence and activity, first, of strictly inorganic structured societies, then of those that simply contain nexuses of living actual occasions without further organization, and finally of those that are governed by a personally ordered subsociety of living occasions or a "soul." At each successive level, there is a proportionate increase in the agency of the structured society as a whole. At the first level, for example, that of inanimate compounds, the atoms are clearly more than random collections of subatomic particles; differences in atomic structure and weight testify to an internal pattern of organization for each of the atoms in the periodic table. Similarly, molecules or ionic compounds are more than simple aggregates of atoms. They, too, exhibit an internal structure and mode of activity that are not simply reducible to the structure and activity of their constituent atoms, taken separately. In both cases, therefore, the atom or molecule, understood as a society or structured environment for the emergence of successive generations of actual occasions, has a profound influence on the internal self-constitution of its constituent occasions. They, in turn, by the consistent way in which they all "prehend" the common element of form within the environment, pass it on relatively unchanged to the next generation of actual occasions. At this level of existence and activity, accordingly, there is a machinelike quality to the total operation that reduces the collective agency of the atom or molecule to an absolute minimum. Yet the constituent occasions clearly behave the way they do because of the societal context or environment within which they exist.

Quite different is the situation within plant and animal cells where, as noted above, an infrastructure of societies of inanimate actual occasions is needed to support nexuses of living occasions which, in turn, through their "originative actions" are "protec-

tive" of those same societies of inanimate occasions. Here the
agency of the cell or structured society as a whole is much more
in evidence. It is, to be sure, still a collective agency, that is, an
agency derivative from the combined individual agencies of both
animate and inanimate actual occasions. But the net effect is the
creation and sustenance of a living being that can act as a unitary
reality vis-à-vis other living beings (other cells). John Cobb, in the
article cited above, is critical of Whitehead's doctrine here because the latter accounts for the phenomenon of life in terms of
two different kinds of activities: the activity of inanimate actual
occasions to account for the order in the cell, the activity of
animate occasions to account for spontaneity.[26] But, from my
perspective, this is proof that Whitehead tacitly accepted the
reality of a collective agency for societies that flows out of the
combined individual agencies of their constituent occasions.
Cobb further notes that Whitehead in *Adventures of Ideas*
seemed to think of life in terms of "the coordination of spontaneities." But this, too, could be interpreted as the collective
agency of the cell or other living organism as a whole rather than
as the special agency of a personally ordered subsociety of living
occasions within the body. To quote another passage from *Adventures of Ideas,* "The living organ of experience is the living body
as a whole."[27] The most obvious explanation of this statement, as
I see it, is that the living body exercises a collective agency from
moment to moment in and through its constituent actual occasions, both animate and inanimate.

Thus, even with reference to the structured society that contains a "regnant" personally ordered society of living occasions, I
would propose that agency is exercised by the structured society
as a whole. The "soul" or regnant subsociety, to be sure, allows
the structured society to be a subject of experience (that is, to
make "decisions") in a way that is impossible either for inanimate physical compounds or for plant life or indeed for primitive
animal organisms lacking a central nervous system. For, in virtue
of the central nervous system, the dominant actual occasion at
any given moment can communicate its "decisions" to all the
subordinate living and nonliving occasions in the body; and
they, in turn, can communicate their response to its successor in
the dominant subsociety.[28] But it is still the structured society as
such, the organism as a whole, that exists and exercises activity.
Otherwise, Whitehead would be guilty of repristinating the Platonic horse-and-rider image of the body-soul correlation. The
body does not exist for the sake of the soul nor the soul for the

sake of the body. Both exist for the sake of the composite that
exercises activity as a unitary whole. In Whiteheadian terms, the
actual occasions constituting the body are immanent within the
successive occasions of the regnant subsociety and vice versa.
Accordingly, whether the dominant occasion is to be found in
this part of the brain or some other part at any given moment is
irrelevant since, wherever it is located, it contributes its individual agency to the collective agency of the organism as a whole.
As Whitehead comments, "The final percipient route of occasions is perhaps some thread of happenings wandering in
'empty' space amid the interstices of the brain."[29] In the end, it is
the organism as a complex structured society that coordinates the
various "spontaneities" within the body and acts as a unitary
whole.

I have laid such heavy stress on this point for two reasons.
First, it allows me to argue against Leclerc that a Whiteheadian
society does not have to be understood as a mere aggregate of
actual occasions. Hence, in those cases where a physical compound (for example, a molecule or a cell) clearly exists as a
unitary reality with an agency proper to its own level of existence, one does not have to say that this is a lower-order substance. One can with equal justification claim that it is a Whiteheadian society exercising a collective agency derivative from
the individual agencies of its constituent actual occasions. Admittedly, from a purely empirical point of view, one could say
that such a physical organism could be interpreted either as a
substance or as a Whiteheadian society. But, in view of my
arguments in the remainder of this chapter that the Whiteheadian notion of society likewise applies to those macroscopic
social realities described by "systems" theory (for example,
human communities and biological environments), then, I contend that one should preferably interpret physical compounds as
societies rather than substances. For in that case one would have
in the notion of society a foundational concept for both the
natural and the social sciences, equivalently the first category of
being for a new cosmology.

Secondly, however, I wish to prevail upon Hartshorne, Cobb
and other Whiteheadians to rethink their customary understanding of the notion of society. In my judgment, they have accepted
at face value Whitehead's statement that agency belongs exclusively to actual occasions and have not asked themselves
sufficiently how Whitehead's philosophy thus avoids the pe-
jorative consequences of metaphysical atomism. In particular, if,

as Whitehead also maintains, "The real actual things that endure are all societies," how can one consistently refrain from attributing to societies some sort of agency if only to account for their perdurance through time as self-sustaining realities? Admittedly, it is a collective agency that is derived exclusively from the fusion of the individual agencies of its constituent parts or members. But is not this the sort of agency that one would logically expect from a society, that is, an intrinsically collective reality? In this respect, Hartshorne's analysis of the "compound individual" in the article cited above is very revealing. He seems to be arguing that in the end only individuals exist (which is, of course, a classical Aristotelian assumption). In fact, at the end of the essay, he argues that the material universe as, so to speak, the "body" of God is a unified or compound individual.[30] As later chapters of this book will make clear, I, on the contrary, hold that the material universe is a structured society that is itself included within the trinitarian society of the three divine persons. Thus the ultimate ontological reality is a society, not an individual entity (not even a compound individual entity). At least on this point, I would certainly endorse the thesis of Jorge Luis Nobo that the universe is a cosmic society of existents (God included) that is initially operative in the concrescence of each actual occasion and then "increased by one" at the termination of the latter's process of self-constitution.[31]

I turn now to a much briefer consideration of still another contemporary cosmology, namely, systems philosophy as worked out by Ervin Laszlo. For, between the Whiteheadian notion of society (at least, as I have reinterpreted it above) and the concept of a "natural system" in Laszlo's scheme there exist in my judgment significant points of comparison. A natural system according to Laszlo is a "nonrandom accumulation of matter-energy, in a region of physical space-time, which is nonrandomly organized into coacting interrelated subsystems or components."[32] In more traditional language, it is a functioning ontological totality of dynamically interrelated parts or members. As such, it is distinguishable from mere aggregates of individual entities, on the one hand, and from artificial systems, that is, humanly constructed machines that in their operation constitute a totality of interrelated parts or members (for example, an automobile or washing machine whose material components are natural systems but whose overall function and design is of human origin). Furthermore, and most importantly for our purposes in this chapter, the notion of a natural system (like that of a White-

headian society) applies not only to organic compounds or substances in the Aristotelian sense of the term, but likewise to
specifically social groups of otherwise relatively self-sufficient
entities (for example, human communities and ecological or
environmental systems).[33]

Given the broad applicability of this concept of natural system,
Laszlo is able to construct an all-embracing cosmology in which
primitive natural systems such as atoms are understood to be
parts of more complex natural systems such as molecules, molecular compounds, crystals, cells, multicellular organisms and
communities of organisms. Such a hierarchically organized
global natural system is then seen as a component in a mega-
system embracing first the solar system, then galaxies and clus-
ters of galaxies, all seen as constituent parts of the astronomical
universe.[34] Naturally, Laszlo is not able to specify the laws or
properties of these higher-order systems; his only point is that,
given a foundational concept like natural system, one should be
able to project in theory an ontological unity for reality as a
whole (apart from God whose existence and activity in the universe is quite consciously not considered by Laszlo). In all of this,
there are obvious parallels with Whitehead's notion of society, at
least as I have presented it here, and with his societal understanding of reality. For Whitehead, too, primitive societies of
actual occasions are grouped into structured societies, that is,
societies composed, not of actual occasions, but of subsocieties;
likewise, these structured societies are themselves components
of ever more complex societies within the unity of our present
cosmic epoch (and perhaps beyond).[35]

Laszlo proposes that within these hierarchically organized
natural systems, different levels of being and activity are distinguished by different patterns of operation for the constituent
systems. That is, a primitive natural system such as an atom
plays an increasingly sophisticated role in the more complex
systems to which it belongs (for example, first in a molecule,
then in a cell, then in an organism, finally in an ecological
system). The capacity to play that more sophisticated role is
latent within the atom from the beginning, but it is activated or
emerges as the atom becomes a member of these more complex
natural systems. As Laszlo comments, "What emerges is not an
unforeseeable novelty, but a new and more complexly organized
dynamic-structural variant of existing types of organization."[36]
With one notable qualification, this is likewise how I understand
the workings of hierarchically ordered societies of actual occa-

sions. That is, the "common element of form" is not imposed from without on the constituent occasions and/or member societies; instead, at each level of existence and activity, it arises out of the dynamic interrelatedness of the occasions active at that level. On the other hand, actual occasions do not possess latent possibilities for further actualization as do atoms in Laszlo's scheme. Rather, as momentary subjects of experience, their only capacity is the power to constitute themselves out of their immediate past environment in all its dynamic interrelatedness. Thus actual occasions within Whitehead's philosophy seem to be more a product of their environment or social context than are atoms in Laszlo's system.

Yet, given this and other minor differences between the cosmologies of Laszlo and Whitehead, they represent, in my judgment, complementary, even supplementary, worldviews. Laszlo's emphasis on natural systems as ontological totalities of interrelated parts or members, for example, forces Whiteheadians to look more carefully at Whitehead's relatively sparse remarks about the nature of societies. The focus by Whiteheadians up to now on the actual occasion as the "building-block" of the universe should perhaps yield to a recognition of the equiprimordial character of societies within a Whiteheadian universe. Not just actual occasions, therefore, but the societies of which they are members are self-sustaining realities with a raison d'être proper to their own level of being and activity.[37] Laszlo and other systems philosophers, on the other hand, through contact with Whitehead's cosmology might well ask themselves whether they need a category like that of actual occasion to describe the ultimate constituents of natural systems. They may not, in other words, be able to content themselves with the statement that in the end there exist only systems.[38] For, systems by definition are ontological totalities of dynamically interrelated parts or members. Hence, one must logically ask what is the nature of these ultimate parts that they readily combine into primitive natural systems.

There is, to be sure, a further metaphysical issue at stake here, namely, the type of agency exercised by an ontological totality. According to Laszlo, only systems exist; hence, only systems exercise agency in line with their specific mode of existence and activity. For Whitehead, on the other hand, actual entities are "the final real things of which the world is made up." Thus only actual entities exercise agency in the strict sense of the word. Yet, earlier in this chapter I argued that Whiteheadian societies likewise exercise agency, albeit a collective agency that comes into being as a result of the dynamic interrelatedness of the individual agencies of their constituent actual entities. Furthermore, this collective agency of the society is sufficiently strong so that the enduring character of the society is imprinted upon the self-constitution of successive generations of actual entities and the society as a whole is able to join with other societies so as to constitute a structured society, a society of subsocieties, at a still higher level of existence and activity.

It might be counterargued, of course, that ontological totalities exercise agency, not indirectly through their constituent parts or members, but rather directly in virtue of their own internal constitution as this or that type of entity. But is this true? By definition, an ontological totality is a unity in plurality of functioning parts or members that thereby have to exercise some type of subordinate agency even to function as a part. All the natural systems within Laszlo's scheme except the most primitive or elementary, for example, are themselves composed of subordinate natural systems that exercise an agency proper to their own reality as a subordinate system even as they contribute to the reality and agency of the higher system. Laszlo, accordingly, does not seem to have thought through all the metaphysical implications of the notion of totality. In particular, he seems to have missed the classical insight of Aristotle into the nature of organic compounds, namely, that a compound is one substance in act but potentially many substances, since each of its material elements is a substance in its own right with an agency proper to its own level of existence and activity.[39] Thus, as Leclerc points out, within an organic compound there "will be one unitary acting, the acting of the compound substance as an actual whole. With reference to this unitary acting of the compound substance, the actings of the constituents will be sub-acts which, but for the unitary substantial form that they share (by virtue of having contributed to it), would themselves be separate individual substances."[40]

Once again, however, it must be emphasized that the "unitary acting" of the compound substance is the collective agency emergent out of the "sub-acts" of its constituent parts. It receives its agency, so to speak, from below, through the interrelated agencies of its constituents; it does not impose its own agency from above, in virtue of a unity and activity proper to itself. The importance of this last point becomes apparent when one reviews the work of another contemporary philosopher, Edward Pols. Using the example of Socrates in Plato's *Phaedo*, who voluntarily drinks the cup of hemlock rather than sacrifice his principles by trying to escape from prison, Pols in *Meditation on a Prisoner* argues that the real agency at work here in Socrates was an "originative act" whereby he deliberately chose to remain faithful to his principles; it is not be be explained in reductional fashion as a by-product of individual cause-effect relationships within his body, notably among the neurons within his brain.[41]

Pols sees himself thereby opposed to two separate groups of scientists. The first group seeks to explain human actions like that of Socrates in terms of the interaction of subatomic particles or whatever else may be conceived as the elementary units of matter. All macroscopic entities, therefore, are simply aggregates of cause-effect relationships among these subatomic units of reality. The second group of scientists, on the other hand, postulates that the existence and activity, first of inanimate compounds (for example, atoms and molecules) and then of plant and animal organisms, cannot be accounted for simply in terms of the interactions of their elementary component parts; rather, these entities exist in virtue of laws appropriate to their individual levels of existence and activity within nature. Equivalently, then, these scientists are "systems" thinkers like Ervin Laszlo.[42]

Pols's objection to this second group of scientists is that they, too, implicitly operate within a deterministic frame of reference. For, they also presuppose that human decisions and other forms of intentional activity can be exhaustively explained in terms of universal laws operative within the body. There is no need in their theory, accordingly, for "originative acts" stemming from the human being as personal agent.[43] As Pols sees it, however, the decision of Socrates to drink the hemlock or any other such decision unifies all the natural processes taking place within the human body, thus integrating and coordinating all the individual cause-effect relationships within the organism. Accordingly, the "laws" referred to by the second group of scientists are at any given moment the collective effect of subacts empowered by the superordinate act, which is the conscious or unconscious decision of the human being at that same moment. Moreover, since the entire life of the human being may be interpreted as his or her primordial originative act, then one may suitably argue that the power of a single originative act such as a decision here and now is derivative from the abiding ontic power of the human being as an enduring personal agent.[44] For that matter, within his scheme the unity of the individual physical organism is itself derived from the transcendent unity of Being.[45]

Pols's implicit model for the relationship of the One to the Many is, then, unmistakably Aristotelian; that is, the unity of a human being or indeed any other complex physical organism is derived from the substantial form that, as the primordial originative act within the body, unifies the subacts at all the subordinate levels of existence and activity. The form, therefore, is active (as noted above, *ein vereinheitlichendes Prinzip*[46]); the material elements by contrast are relatively passive since they receive the form. Given my understanding of a Whiteheadian society, of course, the reverse must be true. That is, actual occasions as the Whiteheadian equivalent of "material elements" are collectively the active principle within the society (the physical compound); the "common element of form," on the other hand, is the passive principle. For even though it functions as the principle of order and stability for successive generations of actual occasions, the form or structure of a Whiteheadian society is derived from the interrelated activities of its constituent occasions. Unlike the Aristotelian substantial form, therefore, it does not actively impose its antecedent unity on constituent parts or members.

At the same time, Pols's description of the all-pervasive presence and activity of an "originative act" within a physical compound, with appropriate qualifications, illuminates what I understand to be the collective agency exercised by a Whiteheadian society in and through the "common element of form" resident in each of its constituent actual occasions:

(a) The "reach" of it [the originative act] is felt throughout a temporal span, but it is not exercised at or from a particular temporal locus. Although its power does not exist in temporal independence of its subordinate levels, it is neither before nor after all the units in them and it is neither before nor after any one of them. (b) It is exercised throughout a spatial region, and its "reach" is felt throughout that region, although by no means uniformly. Although it does not exist in spatial independence of the units of its subordinate levels, it does not exercise itself at or from a particular spatial locus, but only throughout the total volume, though with regions of emphasis here and there; and in this spatial "reach" no temporal span is involved.[47]

As I see it, this is a quite satisfactory description of the way in which a Whiteheadian society exercises a collective agency via the common element of form resident in each of its constituent actual occasions. That is, the form does not exist apart from the occasions, which are thus linked with one another according to a specific structural pattern. It comes into being with a given generation of occasions and ceases to be as they pass out of existence. At the same time, as the all-pervasive form of a given society here and now, it provides the necessary context or environment for the emergence of the next generation of occasions. While these by their interrelated individual agencies will produce still another common element of form, the latter will inevitably resemble quite closely its predecessor and thus guarantee the basic continuity of the society from moment to moment. Finally, while the form is instantiated in all the member occasions, it is more effective in the self-constitution of some of those occasions than of others. Hence, as I shall make clear in chapter 2, this allows one to interpret the common element of form in mathematical terms as a probability distribution and thus to provide for gradual changes within the society as a whole over a period of time.

To conclude, in this chapter I have compared key metaphysical concepts in the thought of many process-oriented philosophers: for example, the concept of substance for Ivor Leclerc; the concept of society for Alfred North Whitehead and two of his more celebrated disciples, Charles Hartshorne and John Cobb; the concept of natural system for Ervin Laszlo; and, finally, the notion of originative act for Edward Pols. While each of these concepts possesses distinct advantages for a process-relational understanding of reality, my conclusion is that the somewhat revised understanding of a Whiteheadian society that I presented above is best equipped to serve as the foundational concept for a contemporary cosmology. It is more comprehensive than Leclerc's notion of substance since it is applicable not only to organic compounds but also to specifically social groups of relatively subsistent entities such as human communities and ecological/ environmental systems. Likewise, better than Pols's notion of an originative act, it makes clear the subtle change in the dynamic relationship between form and matter in the move from classical to process metaphysics. Its superiority to Laszlo's concept of natural system, on the other hand, lies in its perpetuation of a key insight from that same classical tradition. That is, it recognizes that the agency proper to an ontological totality is a collective agency derived from the interlocking character of the agency of the individual parts or members.

Finally, with respect to Hartshorne's and Cobb's understanding of a Whiteheadian society, I would respectfully submit that, while all three of us expand in some measure upon Whitehead's explicit doctrine, my understanding of the nature and function of a society preserves more of what Whitehead actually said about structured societies in *Process and Reality* and elsewhere. That is, the notion of a collective agency seems to be implicit in his remarks about the dynamic interrelationship among actual occasions within inanimate compounds, in his analysis of the interplay between "living" occasions and encompassing inanimate occasions within the cell, and even in his description of the intimate relationship between the "presiding" occasion and the infrastructure of the brain in animal organisms. Within this context, Whitehead's statement that agency belongs exclusively to actual occasions is not wrong but merely incomplete. Whitehead simply failed to mention that these individual agencies fuse into a collective agency for the structured society as a whole.

2

Energy-Events and Fields

In the sixty years or more since quantum mechanics took shape as an autonomous scientific discipline, considerable progress has been made in terms of the mathematics and experimental procedures applicable to this new field of research. But virtually no agreement has been reached on the underlying philosophical issues: namely, the nature of reality at the quantum level and the effect of human measurement on the object under investigation. Accordingly, as Ian Barbour comments: "It is not surprising that the positivist finds in quantum physics support for his conviction that we should *discard all models* [of reality] and treat theories as mere calculational devices for correlating observations. He urges us to give up trying to imagine what goes on between observations."[1] Barbour himself argues that the puzzling results of quantum physics represent a warning against literalism in the use of models rather than cause for their total rejection. Especially since electrons and other quantum-level entities exhibit wavelike and particlelike behavior under different experimental conditions, it is still useful to retain the model of the particle or the wave to describe what is otherwise incomprehensible.

Furthermore, while Barbour concedes that there is a certain complementarity in the function of particle- and wave-models within quantum physics, the notion of complementarity "provides no justification for an uncritical acceptance of dichotomies. It cannot be used to avoid dealing with inconsistencies or to veto the search for unity."[2] In that same spirit, I intend to set forth in this chapter a Whiteheadian (or, perhaps more precisely, neo-Whiteheadian) explanation of the wavelike and particlelike behavior of electrons and other subatomic entities. My explanation, to be sure, will be purely philosophical, not scientific. That is, I will not offer a set of differential equations so as to predict with some measure of accuracy the behavior of these entities in a given context. Rather, I will try to explain how apparently one and the same subatomic reality can exhibit wavelike and particlelike properties.

In brief, my argument will be that the ultimate constituents of material reality are Whiteheadian actual occasions, momentary subjects of experience or, in the language of natural science, localized energy-events that objectify themselves to their successors as wave-patterns of energy within a common field of activity. Whiteheadian "societies," accordingly, should be understood as "fields" for the dynamic interrelation of actual occasions. Here, too, I am evidently setting up an analogy with one of the key concepts in quantum mechanics, even as I fully recognize the elusiveness of this notion of field among scientists themselves. My intention, once again, is simply to provide a theoretical framework for dealing with the philosophical issues raised by quantum mechanics. Furthermore, as I try to make clear in the final third of the chapter, the notion of field is quite useful for analyzing different societal configurations, from the microscopic (for example, the atom) to the macroscopic (for example, human communities). In this way, I will be continuing the argument begun in the previous chapter that "society" rather than "substance" or "natural system" is best suited to serve as the foundational concept of a new cosmology.

To begin, then, according to Whitehead an actual occasion is not simply a self-constituting subject of experience but also, in a sense to be explained below, a "superject" or dynamic projection of itself into the future. Moreover, these two "phases" of its existence are logically, if not temporally, distinct from one another. During the first phase as a subject of experience (which Whitehead himself divides into several subphases), it undergoes a process of concrescence. It becomes itself, in other words, as a unified subject of experience through a series of "prehensions," both physical and conceptual, whereby data from the outside world are organized into a coherent whole. This first phase of its existence is terminated by some sort of implicit "decision," wherein it achieves full actuality as a subject of experience. Then, in the second phase of its existence, it projects its now completed objective reality upon the next generation of concrescing actual occasions. It functions, in other words, as a "superject," thrusting forward into the future of the society (societies) to which it belongs.[3]

But what do these phases have to do with wave-patterns and energy-events? To make the connection clear, I have to elaborate on Whitehead's doctrine of prehensions. Prehensions, says

Whitehead, are not so much cognitive realities as rather feeling-realities. That is, even in higher-order actual occasions such as those constituting temporal consciousness in a human being, past occasions together with the conceptual pattern associated with them are felt before they are cognitively perceived.[4] A *fortiori*, among lower-order actual occasions lacking in consciousness (for example, those making up more primitive forms of animal life, plant life, inanimate reality), preceding occasions and their associated conceptual patterns are simply felt and responded to unconsciously. What, then, is the nature of feeling common to all actual occasions irrespective of their combination into different macroscopic realities? "In the phraseology of physics, this primitive experience is 'vector feeling,' that is to say, feeling from a beyond which is determinate and pointing to a beyond which is yet to be determined."[5] More importantly for our purposes, however, Whitehead also notes that these "pulses of emotion" appear as units of physical energy, that is, as wave-patterns or vibrations. "Thus the transmission of each sensum is associated with its own wavelength."[6] Elsewhere he says: "We shall conceive each primordial element as a vibratory ebb and flow of an underlying energy, or activity . . . an organized system of vibratory streaming of energy."[7] What actual occasions "prehend" from their predecessors, then, are vibratory patterns of energy transmitted through the field (or fields) common to them all.

In terms of the scheme noted above, the first phase in the existence of an actual occasion is that wherein it integrates "pulses of emotion," that is, waves of psychic/physical energy, from antecedent occasions for the purposes of its own concrescence. As noted above, it terminates this process of self-constitution through some kind of implicit decision. It attains, says Whitehead, "satisfaction," the complex unity of feeling at which it had been aiming from the beginning.[8] Moreover, at this juncture, it is "spatialized"; it becomes a localized reality, "a definite, determinate, settled fact."[9] It assumes, in other words, its proper place within what Whitehead calls "the extensive continuum," the all-embracing field of relationships for actual occasions past, present, and future.[10] But this first phase is immediately succeeded by a second phase in which the now determinate actual occasion releases the energy thus contained and shaped by its own process of self-constitution into the extensive continuum for the purpose of shaping and altering the self-constitution of the next generation of actual occasions. This is the phase in which the actual occasion becomes a "superject adding its character to the creativity whereby there is a becoming of entities superseding the one in question."[11] It functions as a superject precisely because it transmits its own complex unity of feeling in the form of a new wave-pattern of psychic/physical energy toward concrescing actual occasions. Only in this way can it contribute its "character" to the overall field of energy out of which the new occasions will arise.

The picture that thus emerges out of a comparison of the two phases with one another is that of a vast field of energy in which localized energy-events are continually taking place in great profusion. Each of these energy-events first draws in multiple sources of energy available to it from the field as a whole, shapes these "vector feelings" in virtue of its own immanent power of self-constitution, and then releases the energy back into the field, albeit with the "character" or pattern of intelligibility imposed by its own unconscious decision. No energy is thereby lost; but the pattern of energy within the field, as a result, is never precisely the same from moment to moment. In the overwhelming number of instances, of course, the individual energy-events basically repeat the pattern already present in the field as a result of previous energy-events. But there is enough alteration of the basic pattern within the field so that one may suitably speak of a process of becoming for the field as a whole, at least in terms of a progressive conversion of potentiality into actuality. In other words, while the energy-events simply happen, the field undergoes various modifications. Or, as Whitehead puts it, "There is a becoming of continuity" because of the progressive changes in the field, "but no continuity of becoming," since each of the energy-events is a separate atomic reality.[12]

In the final third of the chapter, I will take up the issue whether Whiteheadian societies and indeed societies in the common sense understanding of the term (for example, communities, institutions of various kinds) are likewise to be understood as fields of activity, albeit subordinate fields of activity within the all-comprehensive field of the extensive continuum. In this way, the actual entities to be found in a particular region of the space-time continuum could generate among themselves a more specialized common element of form or energy-pattern within that smaller field as well as share in the common element of form for the extensive continuum as a whole (insofar as the latter has been converted from potentiality to actuality in virtue of the world process).

For the moment, however, I wish to draw attention to the reflections of the celebrated philosopher of science Karl Popper in *Quantum Theory and the Schism in Physics*. He argues for a realist as opposed to a strictly instrumentalist understanding of physical reality; that is, against the so-called Copenhagen school of thought, he urges that physicists can achieve knowledge not only of their own measurements of subatomic energy-events, but of the energy-events themselves as independent physical realities. At the same time, he argues against other realists like Albert Einstein, Louis de Broglie, and Erwin Schrödinger that probability theory is grounded in an objective indeterminism within those same energy-events rather than in human ignorance of all the attendant physical conditions.[13] In explaining his own theory wherein physical indeterminism and objective realism are fully compatible, he sketches a "metaphysical dream," which in numerous ways runs parallel to and confirms the interpretation of Whitehead's philosophy presented above.

He begins by noting that in all the various explanations of quantum mechanics the existence of particles is taken for granted. Waves, accordingly, merely determine the frequency with which particles assume a certain state upon repetition of the experiment. Even the so-called quantum field theories "are statistical theories of *particle assemblies:* what they describe are the numbers—or more precisely, the probabilities of a change in the numbers—of the particles in the various possible states."[14] At the same time, he notes that Schrödinger with his novel conception of particles as wave crests or wave packets was not "explaining away" the reality of particles, as his critics assumed, but rather offering a less materialistic explanation of the nature or inner reality of those same particles. His own explanation of subatomic particles is that they are at one and the same time actualizations of certain potentialities and potentialities for further actualizations.[15] In this way, probability theory as applied to subatomic reality is grounded in an objective potentiality of the subatomic particle rather than in human ignorance of all the other physical determinants.

In the special introduction to the long-delayed publication of *Quantum theory and the Schism in Physics* in 1982, Popper refined this idea even further. "Propensities," he suggests, "are properties of neither particles nor photons nor electrons. . . . Propensity statements in physics describe properties of the situation, and are testable if the situation is typical, that is, if it repeats itself."[16] If I understand him aright, what Popper is suggesting in this 1982 emendation of his earlier remarks in the 1950s is that the field set up by the interaction of the particle with its contemporaries is the real bearer of potentialities for the future rather than the particle itself. The particle, after all, is only the momentary actualization of some of the potentialities already existent in the field. Admittedly, together with its contemporaries, it co-determines the configuration of the field for the next set of particle interactions. But it is the field or "situation" which with minor modifications keeps repeating itself as particles are successively created and destroyed in the various interactions. Accordingly, it is the field that serves as the principle of continuity, the bearer of propensities from one moment to the next. Popper himself says that propensities are just as real and objective as particles even though they are described by field equations of a statistical nature. For the statistics do not describe possible fields but rather an existent field with multiple potentialities for future particle-interactions.[17]

So interpreted, Popper's "metaphysical dream" seems to exhibit a remarkable similarity to the interpretation of Whitehead's philosophy that I presented above. That is, in and through the decision whereby it terminates its process of self-constitution, an actual occasion comes to occupy a definite place in the extensive continuum. Thus localized in space and time, it is equivalently a "particle," in Popper's terminology. More precisely, it is a localized energy-event that exhibits the properties of a "particle" in the presence of some macroscopic detection mechanism. In any event, it represents a specific actualization of potentialities already resident in the field out of which it arose. Furthermore, in the next phase of its existence, namely, as a superject, it is a bearer of new potentialities to subsequent actual occasions. The wave-pattern of psychic/physical energy that it releases into the field as a result of the decision as to its self-constitution is felt or "prehended" in a variety of ways by subsequent occasions. Yet here, too, the medium of communication between successive generations of actual occasions is the "society" or field common to them both. The field in question here is, of course, not simply the extensive continuum but all the subfields of activity to which these occasions belong (for example, a physical organism, an entire environment, planetary body). In this way, actual occasions that constitute a definite subsociety or specific field of activity within the extensive continuum give a definite shape or pattern to that field by their interrelated decisions; the field, in turn, serves as the controlling environment for the emergence and self-determination of the next set of actual occasions proper to the organism, environment, or planetary body.

One modest difference between the two approaches, however, remains. Popper interprets the wave-patterns in mathematical terms as statistical probabilities for the repetition of various particle assemblies. Relying upon Whitehead, I propose that wave-patterns are likewise psychic realities, "vector feelings" or "pulses of emotion" transmitted through the encompassing field from one set of actual occasions to another. Fully determinate in themselves, they nevertheless are indeterminate with respect to the way in which they will be incorporated into the self-constitution of the later occasions. In this sense, they represent statistical probabilities for the shape or pattern of the field in the next instant. Thus the "propensities" to which Popper refers possess a psychic/physical reality that he himself apparently never envisioned.[18] Yet such a conclusion follows logically from Whitehead's prior assumption that the ultimate constituents of reality, namely, actual occasions, are subjects of experience, themselves psychophysical realities.

In a paper delivered at a conference on physics and the ultimate significance of time in 1984, the physicist Henry Stapp developed a notion of objective "process time" (as opposed to the subjective measurement of time within the relativity schemes of Einstein), which closely parallels what has been said above. That is, he too argues that physical processes consist of a well-ordered sequence of events in which earlier events condition the possibilities for actualization of later events. The earlier events, in other words, transmit through the space-time continuum objective "tendencies" that narrow the scope of possibilities for subsequent events, and these tendencies can be mathematically calculated using the S-matrix approach to quantum mechanics. He then concludes: "The process formulation of quantum theory contains no explicit dependence on human observers; it allows quantum theory to be regarded as a theory describing the actual unfolding or development of the universe itself, rather than merely a tool by which scientists can, under special conditions, form expectations about their observations."[19]

Stapp is clearly siding here with Karl Popper in advocating a realist as opposed to an instrumentalist epistemology; that is, he too believes that scientific experiment yields knowledge of physical reality in itself, and not simply of human measurements of a reality altogether beyond human comprehension. But he is by implication likewise endorsing the second of Popper's theses, namely, that physical reality is at least partially indeterminate. For, according to his theory, any given situation is replete with possibilities, only one of which will be actualized in the future. Furthermore, the "tendencies" arising out of the present situation merely condition rather than fully determine that which will happen next. Hence, with respect to the future, the quantum process in question is basically undetermined.

Albert Einstein to the end of his life was a determinist in his thinking about the nature of reality. Commenting that God does not play dice, he remained resolutely opposed to the theoretical implications of indeterminism in quantum mechanics. Heinz Pagels, on the contrary, argues: "The very act of attempting to establish determinism produces indeterminism. There is no randomness like quantum randomness. Like us, God plays dice— He, too, knows only the odds."[20] But Pagels does not offer any philosophical justification for that statement; he simply calls attention to the fact that quantum mechanics operates in terms of statistical probabilities rather than with invariant classical laws. The Whiteheadian scheme proposed in this chapter, however, does provide a relatively clear and simple answer to the question why even God cannot know with certainty what will happen in the world of subatomic particles until it actually takes place. In Whitehead's philosophy, a subatomic particle is a society of actual occasions, each of which is a unique subject of experience constituted as such in virtue of its own "decision." The indeterminism in the behavior of the particle is a direct consequence of the process of self-constitution of its constituent actual occasions. Even God cannot know the outcome of this process of self-constitution until it actually takes place because the actual occasion in this stage of its existence is, so to speak, incommunicable. It is not yet a superject and thus not yet an object of feeling and/or knowledge, even for God.

Statistical probabilities, of course, govern a series of events, not individual events. That is, one cannot with certitude know the outcome of an individual event within the series; but one can with the aid of probability theory predict the overall pattern for the series as a whole. Here too Whiteheadian metaphysics provides a philosophical explanation for what is only an enigma on the level of natural science. According to Whitehead, the actual occasions constituting a society are linked together (either spatially, temporally or, most often, both spatially and temporally) by a "common element of form." This common element of form is part of the self-constitution of each constituent actual occasion. Yet each occasion "prehends" it, i.e., internalizes it, in a manner peculiar to itself. The resultant common element of form for the society as a whole, therefore, is equivalently a probability distribution for the entire set of actual occasions. As such, it is nowhere perfectly realized in any of the member occasions. But it represents a sufficient approximation of what has happened in the self-constitution of each constituent occasion that it gives the society as such an objective intelligibility which is quite real. The society is, in other words, an ontological actuality in its own right (albeit in and through the actuality proper to its constituent actual occasions) because of the common element of form which is its unifying principle by way of a probability distribution.

Whitehead himself was apparently reluctant to ascribe ontological actuality to societies over and above the actuality proper to their constituent actual entities because of his basic presupposition that actual entities are "the final real things of which the world is made up."[21] But in his analysis of the Category of Transmutation, he arrives at an understanding of the common element of form as the equivalent of a probability distribution. He notes, for example, in *Process and Reality:* "Transmutation is the way in which the actual world is felt as a community, and is so felt in virtue of its prevalent order. For it arises by reason of the analogies between the various members of the prehended nexus, and eliminates their differences."[22] The key term here is "analogies," since Whitehead thereby implicitly admits that the pattern which binds the constituent actual occasions into a given nexus is not reproduced in each of those entities in exactly the same way. What holds the group of occasions together is a probability distribution whereby some of them reproduce the pattern more faithfully than others but all of them reproduce it with sufficient fidelity that the nexus survives as a functional unity.[23]

Whitehead's focus in this passage and elsewhere, to be sure, is on the unity of the nexus as perceived by a concrescing actual entity. As a result, he elaborates in considerable detail how the concrescing occasion prehends first the analogous physical feelings of the antecedent occasions, then their analogous conceptual feelings derived from their mutual entertainment of the same "eternal object," then perhaps reverted conceptual feelings as a result of its own imaginative activity. In the end the concrescing entity possesses a single conceptual feeling, a single pattern of intelligibility, which thus represents the antecedent nexus of actual occasions as a functioning unity rather than as a mere aggregate of separate individuals.[24] But it is clear that chaos would result unless the unity perceived by the concrescing occasion more or less corresponded to the unity objectively present in the antecedent nexus. Otherwise, there would be no continuity in the nexuses or societies of actual occasions from moment to moment. For the societal unity (unities) that the concrescing occasion is co-constituting with its contemporaries is directly dependent upon all of them more or less faithfully reproducing in their individual self-constitutions the pattern of intelligibility, the complex eternal object or common element of form, exhibited by their immediate predecessors. As Whitehead comments: "A high-grade percipient is necessarily an occasion in the historic route of an enduring object. If this route is to propagate itself successfully into the future, it is above all things necessary that its decisions in the immediate occasion should have the closest relevance to the concurrent happenings among contemporary occasions."[25]

The point of this discussion, of course, is not to introduce the reader to the more subtle details of Whitehead's system, but to indicate how that same system provides a philosophical explanation for what otherwise is an enigma for natural science, namely, how random events, above all on the level of subatomic particles but likewise in the world of macroscopic realities, produce through their dynamic interrelation patterns of intelligibility that are more or less invariant. The answer, says Whitehead, can only lie in the presupposition that the ultimate constituents of reality are momentary subjects of experience that effect their individual self-constitution through an immanent "decision" and which indirectly co-constitute with their contemporaries the verifiable objective unities of human experience (for example, atoms, molecules, cells, organisms, societies in the macroscopic sense, environments and ecosystems). The sticking point for the natural scientist, however, is that one must then unequivocally reject what Whitehead calls scientific materialism, that is, the implicit assumption that the ultimate constituents of material reality are themselves bits of matter, however attenuated.[26] This strikes many natural scientists as unreasonable even though they readily accept with Einstein the basic convertibility of matter with energy. Energy, they seem to say, is still a form of matter that is empirically measurable.

Yet, if matter is basically convertible with energy, then it is clearly not a passive underlying "stuff" out of which the things of this world are fashioned but the dynamic source of all movement and activity in the world. Capitalizing on this insight, Murray Code comments that matter should be understood as the "capacity to make and register differences."[27] An entity is material, then, to the extent that its interactions with other (material) entities make or at least register a measurable difference. But, given this understanding of matter, the actual occasions, first as subjects of experience that draw upon their environment for their self-constitution and then as "superjects" that actively impact upon that same environment, should be understood as material entities. Admittedly, they are not inert bits of matter in the traditional sense; but neither are the "particles" of high-energy physics simply inert bits of matter that collide with one another in a variety of ways. Physicists, accordingly, might well ask themselves whether their philosophical understanding of matter is basically compatible with the sophistication of their research methods in science.

Here, however, is where the deeper problem may well lie. Many physicists and mathematicians do not appear at all concerned about the philosophical implications of their work. Their underlying assumption seems to be that it is really not important to know the inner nature of the reality that one is dealing with, provided that one's statistical calculations are confirmed by carefully controlled physical experiments. Since the "world" of quantum mechanics is so obviously removed from the world of ordinary human life, it seems more sensible to ignore the philosophical implications of what one is doing and simply concentrate on the results of one's research. The price that one pays for such a decision, however, is very high. For a strictly instrumentalist approach to reality on the part of natural scientists inevitably tends to align them and their work with the pragmatic, results-oriented mentality of technicians and at the same time subtly to distance them from the value-oriented mentality of other academicians working in the humanities and, to some extent, the social sciences. Thus, if only to reintegrate the natural sciences with the humanities and the social sciences within the world of academe, a new philosophical understanding of reality is desperately needed.[28]

I turn now to the second hypothesis of this chapter, namely, that societies, both in the technical Whiteheadian sense and in the common sense understanding of the term (communities of various kinds and institutions, for example) should be understood as overlapping energy fields, each with an intelligible pattern corresponding to the energy-events (concrescence of actual occasions) taking place within it. As already noted in this chapter, there is a tendency among contemporary physicists to think of subatomic reality at least partly in terms of interacting fields of energy. But can this concept be applied to organic and inorganic compounds, to the persons and things of ordinary experience? Furthermore, is it applicable to supraindividual realities, such as communities and environments? To respond to these questions, I will first determine in what sense Whitehead himself thought of societies as fields of activity and then make some further deductions of my own.

In the chapter entitled "Order of Nature" in *Process and Reality*, Whitehead proposes, first of all, that "a society is, for each of its members, an environment with some element of order in it, persisting by reason of the genetic relations between its own members."[29]

The crucial word here is *environment*. It would seem to be roughly equivalent to "field," especially since the environment has an "element of order" in it much akin to the pattern of intelligibility that I proposed for fields in the preceding paragraph. In both cases, the element of order or pattern of intelligibility is due to the genetic interrelatedness of the member actual entities. Furthermore, Whitehead goes on to say, "Every society must be considered with its background of a wider environment of actual entities, which also contribute their objectifications to which the members of the society must conform."[30] This implies that there are fields within fields, such that actual entities that are members of more specialized fields must likewise conform to the laws governing the behavior of actual entities in less specialized but more comprehensive fields. The actual entities in my body, for example, must conform to the laws governing the behavior of actual entities everywhere in the universe as well as be subject to the more specialized laws governing the human body in general and me as a particular human being.

This, however, is to anticipate what I shall say momentarily by way of explanation of the different kinds of fields within the Whiteheadian universe. For the moment, it is sufficient to note that, without using the precise term, Whitehead conceives societies in terms of fields governed by different patterns of order and/or intelligibility. Furthermore, in specifying how that pattern of intelligibility arises within a given field, Whitehead indicates the interdependence of the field with its "defining characteristic" on the interplay of the constituent actual occasions and vice versa:

The causal laws which dominate a social environment are the product of the defining characteristic of that society. But the society is only efficient through its individual members. Thus in a society, the members can only exist by reason of the laws which dominate the society, and the laws only come into being by reason of the analogous characters of the members of the society.[31]

Hence, the society, understood as the ongoing field of activity or social environment, preserves the pattern of interrelatedness for successive generations of actual occasions. The occasions themselves, to be sure, by their de facto interrelatedness from moment to moment may gradually modify that pattern. But it still remains true that, while actual occasions come and go, societies endure. The field of activity remains constant even though its constituents are continually renewed.

As noted above, the most comprehensive society or field of activity for Whitehead is the extensive continuum, the overall scheme of relatedness within which past actual occasions came into being, present occasions are currently concrescing, and future occasions will inevitably take their place. The next most comprehensive field of activity is what Whitehead calls the geometrical society proper to our cosmic epoch, in virtue of which straight lines and other geometrical properties of actual occasions in their interrelatedness are defined. Thirdly, there is the society of electromagnetic occasions that corresponds to the electromagnetic field in physics. Finally, given the quasi-infinite number of electronic and protonic actual occasions thereby in dynamic interrelation, there arise first energy-waves, then particulate matter in such forms as individual electrons and protons, atoms, molecules, inorganic bodies, cells, and organic bodies. [32] In each case, actual occasions that are members of more complex fields of activity (for example, an animal body) likewise belong to a whole series of supportive societies or fields of activity with more comprehensive membership (that is, the extensive continuum, the geometrical society, the society of electromagnetic occasions) and obey the causal laws governing the activity of actual occasions within those same parameters.

Given this understanding of Whiteheadian societies as successively ordered and, to some extent at least, overlapping fields of activity, can one apply this concept to the understanding both of individual entities, organic and inorganic, and of specifically social realities, such as communities and environments? It would seem relatively easy to describe communities and physical environments as fields of activity. In fact, as I have pointed out elsewhere, [33] the major problem with an appropriate metaphysical understanding of human community in the past has been the lack of a category other than individual substance to describe their existence and mode of operation. That is, philosophers have tended to conceive communities either in terms of a supraindividual substance or as an aggregate of autonomous individuals. In the first case, there is the danger of collectivist or totalitarian ways of thinking; in the second case, the equally grave danger of overly individualistic or laissez-faire patterns of thought. Understanding a community as a field of activity for its constituent members, however, seems to avoid both these dangers. On the one hand, the community is not a supraindividual entity that can subordinate its members as ontological "accidents," so to speak, to its own substantial reality. It exists as a field of activity only because its human members are in ongoing dynamic relation to one another. On the other hand, as noted above, the field endures as individual members come and go. The field is the bearer of the ongoing pattern of intelligible relations that is characteristic of one community rather than another. At least in the larger civil communities, it manifests itself in such things as language, laws, customs, various economic, and political and cultural arrangements. But, even in smaller local communities, the field preserves the historical identity or the character of the group as individual members come and go with the passage of time.

Much the same argument could be made for the description of environments or ecosystems as fields of activity for the various individual entities, organic and inorganic, existing within them. An environment comes into being and perdures only because of the dynamic interrelation of its individual constituents. Moreover, it gradually changes character as the relations of individual entities with one another undergo modification over a period of time. But, much like a civil community, it provides a principle of continuity and stability for those same changes. As noted above, the common element of form or basic pattern of intelligibility for such a field of activity becomes operative through a probability distribution. In consequence, even though there may be dramatic changes taking place in one area of the environment, there will not be major changes in the environment as a whole until, statistically speaking, every other area of the environment is similarly affected.

When one asks oneself, however, whether individual substances, both organic and inorganic, can be considered fields of activity with a dominant pattern of intelligibility, the response has to be more nuanced. First of all, Whitehead talks about the difference between democratically and monarchically organized structured societies. As already noted in chapter 1, structured societies are societies composed, not of actual occasions directly, but rather of subordinate societies that may or may not be immediately constituted by actual occasions. Given the fact that an individual electron or proton is already a society of actual occasions, all the "objects" of macroscopic experience (for example, rocks, plants, and animals) are highly complex structured societies. Among structured societies, however, there is a major difference between democratically and monarchically organized societies. A democratically organized society, as the word itself suggests, is a group of actual occasions (or subsocieties) perduring in space and time with a common element of form or pattern of intelligibility but without a central focus or internal principle of organization other than the common element of form itself present in the self-constitution of all the members.[34] The actual occasions making up a rock, for example, have all prehended or internalized the pattern of intelligibility that binds them together as this rock in this place and at this time. But none of the actual occasions (or subsocieties to which it belongs) plays a greater organizing role within the whole than any of the other entities (subsocieties). They are a functioning democracy within the structured society or complex field of activity which is this rock. Monarchically organized structured societies, on the other hand, presuppose an internal principle of organization, what Whitehead calls a "regnant nexus" or, more often "regnant nexūs," which are the basis for originality and novelty within the organism.[35] In this sense, the other subsocieties with their constituent occasions subserve the existence and functioning of the regnant nexuses even as the latter through their specialized activity promote the overall well-being of the structured society.

Much more will be said on this subject in the next chapter when I take up the issue of "dissipative structures" and the principle of entropy. For now, it is only important to note how the notion of field of activity has to be adjusted, depending upon whether one is thinking of democratically or monarchically organized structured societies. In both cases, there is a field of activity constituted by actual occasions in dynamic interrelation; likewise, in both cases, there is a common element of form or dominant pattern of intelligibility. The difference lies, as noted above, in whether or not there is an internal principle of organization within the field whereby the pattern is first modified within one subsociety and then in its modified form communicated to all the other subsocieties with their constituent actual occasions within the structured society or field of activity as a whole. This is the function of the regnant nexuses or, in higher-order animals, of the personally ordered society of actual occasions called the soul. As Whitehead says with respect to the human soul: "This culmination of bodily life transmits itself as an element of novelty throughout the avenues of the body. Its sole use to the body is its vivid originality; it is the organ of novelty."[36]

Yet in the final analysis, whether a field of activity is democratically or monarchically organized would seem to be relatively unimportant for its existence and operation simply as a field, provided that the field in either case holds together as a functioning unity in virtue of a common element of form. As Whitehead comments, "A society is, for each of its members, an environment with some element of order in it, persisting by reason of the genetic relations between its own members."[37] How the common element of form comes into being and is transmitted to successive generations of actual occasions is ultimately less important than the fact that it exists to constitute a group of occasions as a society in the first place.

The only final objection to the equation of organic and inorganic entities with fields of activity dominated by a common element of form is that these entities do not look like fields of activity. They look like "things," that is, solid, relatively impermeable material realities with purely external relations to one another. In response, all one can say is that appearances deceive. Natural science has already verified that material bodies, both organic and inorganic, are at any given moment a complex network of subatomic energy-events. What is this network, however, but a field of activity such as I have described in this chapter? Most scientists, to be sure, are apparently not yet ready to admit that the subatomic energy-events are the effect of the "decisions" of momentary subjects of experience called actual entities or actual occasions. But this, as I see it, is something which may well be achieved over a period of time as the interdisciplinary value of an overarching metaphysical scheme such as that proposed by Whitehead begins to take hold in the minds of these same natural scientists. The far bigger step is the one already achieved by the scientific community, namely, to admit that the deliverances of the senses to human consciousness represent the end product of an enormously complex process of abstraction and simplification of profuse elementary data. What we see, hear, feel, smell, and taste does indeed correspond to reality but not in the simplistic manner understood in previous centuries.[38] In that sense, the battle over the "substantiality" of the physical world has already been fought and definitively settled within the scientific community.

To sum up, then, the Whiteheadian notion of society, when understood as an ongoing field of activity for successive generations of actual occasions, appears initially well suited to serve as a foundational concept for a new cosmology. For, on the one hand, it seems to be compatible with the results of scientific research done on the submicroscopic level, namely, in quantum mechanics. On the other hand, a preliminary survey of its adaptability to higher-level forms of social organization suggests that it might well be functional there also. Chapter 3 will carry this investigation into the realms of chemistry and biology.

3

Entropy and Dissipative Structures

Two of the most far-reaching scientific hypotheses of the nine-teenth century were surely the formulation of the two laws of thermodynamics by Rudolph Clausius in 1865 and the theory of evolution proposed by Charles Darwin in 1859. Yet, while shar-ing a common assumption, namely, the irreversibility of time, they seemed to draw totally different conclusions with respect to the future of life on this earth. Clausius argued that, even though the total amount of energy in the world remains constant, the amount of energy that is useable for further work is constantly diminishing. Hence, our solar system, indeed, the entire uni-verse, is slowly undergoing "heat death" as the amount of en-tropy within the "system" continues to increase. Darwin, on the other hand, argued that with the passage of time there has taken place on the earth a gradual evolution from more simple to more complex forms of life. Following this line of thought, one would conclude that there exist vast, still unused potentialities for pro-liferation and further diversification of the various branches on the Tree of Life. Yet such proliferation and diversification of life forms will demand as a precondition large concentrations of energy organized into highly complex patterns of events and activities. How, then, can our world be simultaneously "winding up" and "winding down," that is, advancing to new levels of organization and complexity even as it continues to move toward a condition of maximum entropy in which there will be no effective organization or structure even on the atomic level but only the random interplay of subatomic particles?

In their recently published work, *Order Out of Chaos*, Ilya Prigogine and Isabelle Stengers offer a response to this question, which, though tentative and incomplete, is nevertheless thought-provoking.[1] In book one, they maintain that the principles of classical dynamics as articulated in Newton's *Principia* and elsewhere worked as well as they did for roughly three hundred years because they basically abstracted from the complexities of nature as it really exists in order to present an idealized picture of nature as it ought to exist. Some of these abstractions, for example, the reversibility of changes within a dynamic system and, therefore, the convertibility of past and future within that same system, were eventually challenged in the nineteenth century by the newly founded science of thermodynamics. An overview of the progressive discoveries in thermodynamics occupies the second part of the book. In that same section, moreover, they make clear how irreversible processes in chemistry and molecular biology often bring about a higher stage of order and self-organization through initially random "fluctuations" within the system at an earlier stage of development. Thus, within "dissipative structures," that is, chemical and biological systems that flourish in open-ended, far-from-equilibrium conditions, the principle of entropy can often produce order rather than disorder.

Finally, in the third and concluding part of their book, they raise the issue of irreversible processes at the atomic and subatomic levels of activity. Here they propose that, while stable dynamic systems at these levels seem to function in accord with the principles of classical dynamics, unstable systems whose activity can only be measured in terms of statistical probabilities are necessarily interpreted in terms of irreversible processes. The second law of thermodynamics, in other words, acts as a selection principle whereby physical experimentation within a system is invariably from known initial conditions in the present to randomness in the future, rather than from known initial conditions to randomness in the past. Randomness thus implies irreversibility or the "arrow of time" in the direction of the future, thus exposing the idealization inherent in purely mathematical projections of a system moving from a known present to randomness in the past.

In the present chapter, I will comment on the three divisions of *Order out of Chaos* in the following manner. First, I will indicate that the argument of Prigogine and Stengers with respect to the abstractive nature of classical dynamics in book one was actually anticipated by Alfred North Whitehead fifty years earlier in *Science and the Modern World* and other texts. Then I will try to show how the spontaneous self-organization of "dissipative structures" as set forth by Prigogine and Stengers in book two can be explained by reference to Whitehead's doctrine of "entirely living" nexuses within structured societies and of personally ordered societies within "entirely living" nexuses. This will have the effect of further explaining my own understanding of White-headian societies, even as I make clear why, in my judgment, Whitehead's metaphysics provides the theoretical underpinning for the Prigogine-Stengers hypothesis of "order through fluctuations." Finally, in the last part of the chapter, I will deal with the issue whether, as a matter of fact, there are any reversible processes at all within nature. Prigogine and Stengers seem to allow for this possibility within relatively stable dynamic systems; my own contention will be that all *systems* are time-bound or irreversible even though individual *processes* within a given system may be relatively time-independent and in that sense appear reversible. But this is an illusion rather than a fact; all processes in nature involve the undirectional passage of time.

To begin, then, Whitehead in *Science and the Modern World* called attention to the fact that in the seventeenth century, the "age of genius," as he calls it, all the great physicists and nearly all the great philosophers were likewise mathematicians; hence, mathematics with its inherent capacity for the creation of abstract schemes of thought was a key tool in the hands of both physicists and philosophers for the understanding of nature.[2] The net result, however, was that both philosophers and physicists fell into what Whitehead calls the fallacy of misplaced concreteness; that is, they mistook their abstractions from reality in the form of mathematical formulas and physical laws for the full description of the reality (realities) in question.[3] To be specific, philosophers and physicists of that period took over uncritically the common sense assumption that physical reality is made up of configurations of matter with simple location in space and time. What is here is not there, that is, somewhere else. The relations of material entities to one another, then, are purely external. Change takes place in terms of the movement of these entities from one location in space and time to another under the influence of various external forces (for example, gravity), which can be mathematically calculated and formulated as a general principle applicable to all entities everywhere. Time, therefore, is not an essential component in this abstractive scheme since time itself is understood as a linear succession of instants, each of which is, mathematically speaking, a duplicate of its predecessor and successor. Qualitative change is either illusory or, in any case, a secondary effect of quantifiably measurable exchanges between material entities in spatio-temporal collocation.

Whitehead's comment on this approach to reality so characteristic of science and philosophy in the seventeenth and eighteenth centuries in Western Europe is illuminating:

> The advantage of confining attention to a definite group of abstractions, is that you confine your thoughts to clear-cut definite things, with clear-cut definite relations. Accordingly, if you have a logical head, you can deduce a variety of conclusions respecting the relationships between these abstract entities. Furthermore, if the abstractions are well-founded, that is to say, if they do not abstract from everything that is important in experience, the scientific thought which confines itself to these abstractions will arrive at a variety of important truths relating to our experience of nature.[4]

Thus the dramatic discoveries, above all, in the fields of physics and chemistry in the seventeenth and eighteenth centuries made it all but impossible to question the worldview or set of philosophical assumptions about the nature of reality implicit in this methodology. At the same time, humanistically oriented thinkers and writers in those days found it impossible to discount the qualitative richness of their human experience even in the face of the manifest discoveries of science. As a result, they effectively created a separate world of discourse, one shaped by insights from the humanities (for example, art and literature) rather than from the sciences. But, as Whitehead notes, they thereby indirectly contributed to the dualism of mind *versus* matter in Western thought that was originally proposed by René Descartes.[5] The only way to overcome this dichotomy, in Whitehead's judgment, is to espouse a philosophy of organism (or "organic mechanism") whereby the concrete enduring entities are all organisms and even submicroscopic entities such as electrons behave as they do in virtue of the overall organic plan of the situation in which they find themselves.[6]

As I see it, basically this same line of thought is presented in book one of *Order out of Chaos*. That is, Prigogine and Stengers, without making specific reference to the Whiteheadian notion of the fallacy of misplaced concreteness, nevertheless call attention to the "strangeness" of the world described by classical dynamics.

> Everyone is familiar with the absurd effects produced by projecting a film backward—the sight of a match being regenerated by its flame, broken ink pots that reassemble and return to a tabletop after the ink has poured back into them, branches that grow young again and turn

into fresh shoots. In the world of classical dynamics, such events are considered to be just as likely as the normal ones.[7]

According to classical dynamics, if the velocities of all the points of a system are reversed, then the system will retrace all the states it went through during the previous change; in effect, it will go backward in time. But can this be accomplished except in an ideally isolated system, that is, except in abstraction from the concrete circumstances of life?

The authors likewise point out that, even though classical dynamics represented a triumph of human reason, the world-view that it implicitly set forth was profoundly alienating to the human spirit. Classical dynamics "revealed to men a dead, passive nature, a nature that behaves as an automaton which, once programed, continues to follow the rules inscribed in the program. In this sense, the dialogue with nature isolated man from nature instead of bringing him closer to it."[8] Accordingly, those who took refuge from the mechanistic approach of science in the world of arts and letters were tempted to abandon "reason" in favor of pure spontaneity and other thinly disguised forms of irrational behavior.[9] Finally, at the end of book one they cite Henri Bergson and Whitehead as philosophers who recognized the dangers in this dichotomy between science and the humanities and constructed philosophical systems to bridge the gap.

As already noted, book two of *Order out of Chaos* is initially an overview of the history of the science of thermodynamics. But Prigogine and Stengers likewise have in mind gradually to set forth their own hypothesis that in many cases the principle of entropy is productive of order rather than disorder. Their focus is on dissipative structures, that is, chemical or biological systems that are "far from equilibrium" by reason of fluctuations taking place internally or through interaction with the environment. The order within the existing system is breaking down; but, paradoxically, a new order, a higher level of self-organization for the system as a whole, is gradually taking shape. At critical stages in this process, bifurcations take place in the sense that the system "chooses" one of two possible avenues of development. This "choice" may be assisted by influences from the external environment or it may be due to factors native to the system in its present stage of development. But, in either case, there is no way absolutely to predict the outcome of this "choice" until it happens. They conclude:

A system far from equilibrium may be described as organized not because it realizes a plan alien to elementary activities, or transcending them, but, on the contrary, because the amplification of a microscopic fluctuation occurring at the "right moment" resulted in favoring one reaction path over a number of other equally possible paths. Under certain circumstances, therefore, the role played by individual behavior can be decisive.[10]

Processes of self-organization in far-from-equilibrium states, accordingly, correspond to a delicate balance between chance and necessity. Near a bifurcation, fluctuations or other random elements within the system play a decisive role; between bifurcations, the system operates more along deterministic lines.

Still another factor to be considered is that a fluctuation that sets up a new pattern or level of self-organization is initially localized in one part of the system and only by degrees establishes itself throughout the system. In effect, this means that the molecules or other component parts "communicate" with one another so as to distribute the fluctuation within the entire system. Similarly, if the localized fluctuation does not succeed in propagating itself through the entire system, the molecules may be said implicitly to have cooperated in protecting the stability of the system in its present state. In either case, some sort of informal communication between the component parts of a chemical or biological system in a far-from-equilibrium state must be assumed since only in virtue of acting as a unitary whole will the system either regain its antecedent stability or move on to a higher level of self-organization. What makes this situation even more remarkable, of course, is that molecules in relatively stable chemical or biological systems (those at equilibrium or near equilibrium) behave essentially as entities that ignore one another's presence and activity. Prigogine and Stengers refer to them as "hypnons" or "sleepwalkers," so as to contrast them with molecules within systems in a far-from-equilibrium state that, as already indicated, actively communicate with one another.[11]

The authors, naturally, as practicing scientists rather than professional philosophers, do not offer a metaphysical explanation for the behavior of molecules in these different states. Their only objective is to establish the hypothesis that the second law of thermodynamics, that is, the principle of entropy, often gives rise to higher forms of order after a period of initial disorder. In my judgment, however, an appropriate metaphysical explanation for this phenomenon is to be found in Whitehead's doctrine of entirely living nexuses. This is not to say that Whitehead expressly had in mind what Prigogine and Stengers refer to as dissipative structures, but only to infer that his metaphysical categories, properly understood and applied, shed considerable light on what is happening from a strictly scientific point of view. In the following paragraphs, accordingly, I will first present Whitehead's docrine on structured societies and then indicate its applicability to the phenomenon of dissipative structures.

Whitehead notes, first of all, that a society may be more or less stable with reference to changes taking place in its environment.[12] That is, if it can retain its basic structure despite these changes, it is stable; if it loses its basic pattern of organization as a result of the changes, it is unstable. He then adds that the challenge for "Nature" is to produce societies that are flexible enough to absorb changes taking place in the environment and yet stable enough to survive in a modified state. He cites two strategies or techniques available to societies to achieve that goal. "One way is by eliciting a massive average objectification of a nexus, while eliminating the detailed diversities of the various members of the nexus in question."[13] The actual occasions constituting the society, in other words, prehend from their predecessors and then transmit to their successors a common element of form or pattern of intelligibility for the society as a whole that is fixed and unchanging, hence, completely stable, from moment to moment. Minor diversities of prehension and transmission on the part of the member actual occasions are ignored in favor of a statistical average that becomes the governing principle of operation for the society as a whole.[14] "The second way of solving the problem is by an initiative in conceptual prehensions, i.e., in appetition."[15] That is, the occasions constitutive of the society jointly prehend novel elements within the environment and integrate them within their individual processes of concrescence. Thus, through the individual processes of concrescence for its member occasions, the society as a whole adjusts to a new situation within its environment.

Yet, very much as Prigogine and Stengers noted with respect to fluctuations within dissipative structures, the adaptation to novel elements in the environment does not happen simultaneously throughout the society. It is initially a localized phenomenon that only gradually becomes distributed among all the constituent actual occasions. The way in which this distribution takes place may be explained as follows. Within a structured society such as those in question here, there are different sub-groups or nexuses of actual occasions with diverse charac-teristics. The overwhelming majority of occasions, for example, belong to nexuses that are inorganic in character. These occa-sions normally transmit unchanged to their successors a pattern of order and intelligibility that they inherited from their prede-cessors. But other occasions within the structured society exhibit a higher degree of originality or adaptability to the environment within their individual processes of concrescence. These occa-sions form one or more "entirely living" nexuses within the structured society. As such, they represent what Prigogine and Stengers call a "nucleation mechanism" for the spread of a new pattern of order and intelligibility (for Prigogine and Stengers, a new fluctuation) throughout the entire structured society (chemi-cal or biological system).[16]

That is, the actual occasions constitutive of the inorganic nex-uses prehend the novelty and originality exhibited by the actual occasions belonging to the "entirely living" nexuses and over a period of time incorporate the new pattern of existence and activity into their own processes of concrescence. This does not happen all at once since by definition a nexus or grouping of living actual occasions is itself somewhat unstable. The new pattern that a given set of living occasions transmits thus does not become fixed and certain until it is appropriated by the actual occasions constitutive of the inorganic nexuses. In this way, as Whitehead notes, the "originative actions" of the living occasions within a structured society acquire meaning and, above all, permanence only if those elements of novelty are communicated to the structured society as a whole with all its inorganic subsocieties. On the other hand, without the presence and activity of such loosely organized sets of living occasions within the structured society, development in the direction of life or, in any case, a higher stage of self-organization would be impossible.[17]

In the same way that life depends upon nonlife, that is, living actual occasions upon inorganic actual occasions organized ac-cording to certain patterns, so consciousness in the higher-level animal organisms depends upon the infrastrucure of living occa-sions for its existence and activity. That is, while the living occasions in themselves do not constitute a society, they provide the basis for the emergence of a new kind of society that White-head calls the "soul" or a "living person," that is, a personally ordered society that at least intermittently achieves consciousness.[18] Not every personally ordered society, of course, is conscious. But to sustain even a minimum degree of consciousness, a group of occasions have to be personally ordered, that is, inherit from one another in unidirectional fashion.[19] What distinguishes a conscious, personally ordered society of occasions from one that is nonconscious is the fact that for the former the inheritance consists primarily of "hybrid" prehensions, that is, prehensions of the *mentality* of the preceding occasion as opposed to its physical characteristics. In this way, a governing mentality is carried over from one occasion to another within the series, albeit with suitable modifications in each instance, and this is what is commonly known as consciousness.[20]

Consciousness, of course, is not an activity that is exercised in and for itself. As noted above, it is an intermittent function of the dominant subsociety within the physical organism, namely, the soul. It is interrupted by sleep and even during waking hours is exercised with varying degrees of intensity. But it is in any case the organ of central direction and control within the animal body. As Whitehead comments: "It is by reason of the body, with its miracle of order, that the treasures of the past environment are poured into the living occasion [that is, the actual occasion constituting the soul at any given instant]. . . . In its turn, this culmination of bodily life transmits itself as an element of novelty throughout the avenues of the body. Its sole use to the body is its vivid originality; it is the organ of novelty."[21] Living actual occasions, to be sure, are the "organ of novelty" among the inorganic occasions upon which they depend for their existence and activity. But the pattern of order transmitted by living occasions to the inorganic occasions is somewhat sporadic and intermittent since living occasions, as noted earlier, do not constitute as such a society with a well-defined pattern of inheritance. The soul, on the other hand, as a personally ordered society of occasions, sustains this well-defined pattern of inheritance even as it, too, functions as an organ of novelty. "Thus life is a passage from physical order to pure mental originality, and from pure mental originality to canalized mental originality."[22] Without such canalization in virtue of the presence and activity of the soul within the body, the animal organism as a whole could not survive.

What, then, is to be said by way of comparison between the metaphysical scheme of Whitehead and the hypothesis of "order through fluctuations" espoused by Prigogine and Stengers? First, they all see the necessity for a physical, chemical, or biological system (in Whitehead's terminology, a society or structured field of activity) to maintain stability in the presence of change. Without a basic stability for the system as a whole, changes will produce disorder leading to the breakdown of the existing system rather than a higher level of self-organization ending in the creation of a new system. Whitehead goes on to say that for societies of lesser complexity change is effectively dealt with by being factored out or ignored. As noted above, minor diversities of prehension and transmission on the part of the member actual occasions are set aside in favor of a statistical average that becomes the common element of form or operational principle for the society as a whole. The metaphysical category in question here is that of transmutation. While it is operative at all levels of societal organization, it is especially active in the self-constitution of inanimate realities, for example, crystals, rocks, planets, and suns.[23] As I see it, this level of societal organization within Whitehead's scheme corresponds more or less perfectly to what Prigogine and Stengers refer to as physical and chemical systems at equilibrium or near equilibrium. In their judgment, it will be remembered, the component parts of such systems behave like "hypnons" or "sleepwalkers" vis-à-vis one another, since they virtually ignore each other's presence and activity. In a word, change or novelty is factored out in favor of the ongoing stability of the system as a whole.

Societies (or fields) of greater complexity, however, says Whitehead, deal with the issue of stability in the presence of change or novelty through an initiative in conceptual prehension either on the part of living occasions within societies of inorganic actual occasions or through the new reality of a personally ordered society or "soul" for the organism as a whole. In either case, what originates in some localized part of the total organism has to be communicated effectively to all the other subsocieties of actual occasions if it is to perdure, indeed, if the structured society as a whole is to survive and flourish in the face of changes taking place in the environment. Admittedly, the speed of communication is much greater if the physical organism is sufficiently well developed to support a soul or personally ordered society of occasions as its organ of central direction and control. But, on the other hand, the challenges (or threats) to the stability of the organism are so much greater at this higher level of self-organization.

In any event, these more complex structured societies within

Whitehead's frame of reference correspond, as far as I can judge, to what Prigogine and Stengers refer to as dissipative structures.[24] Here, too, however, communication between the component parts of the system is absolutely indispensable. The molecules or other components can no longer behave like "hypnons" vis-à-vis one another. Instead, they must actively communicate so as either to resist the fluctuations coming from some localized part of the system or to cooperate in their dissemination through the entire system. As Prigogine and Stengers comment, "There is competition between stabilization through communication and instability through fluctuations. The outcome of that competition determines the threshold of stability."[25]

In brief, then, allowing for differences of terminology, Whitehead's scheme for the organization of complex structured societies and Prigogine and Stenger's discussion of dissipative structures seem to reinforce one another. To be specific, both the philosopher and the two natural scientists seem to be saying from different perspectives that nondeterministic processes, that is, processes in which spontaneity and "choice," at least at intervals, play a key role in determining the direction and final outcome of the operation, are the rule rather than the exception at a certain level of self-organization within nature. Moreover, from that point on, as a result of such spontaneity and choice on the part of the components, natural processes are unquestionably irreversible; they proceed inexorably forward in time. As a result, they have to be understood and controlled in terms of thermodynamics with the law of entropy as its key operative principle. This, however, does not spell disaster but rather unprecedented opportunity for the evolutionary process as a whole since, as Prigogine and Stengers point out again and again, fluctuations (disorder) within an existing system paradoxically can give rise to higher levels of self-organization (order) within the system or to a new system altogether. Whitehead seems to make the same point when he says in Process and Reality, "The growth of a complex structured society exemplifies the general purpose pervading nature."[26] Moreover, the whole thrust of his argument both here and elsewhere is to the effect that literally every process within nature is time-bound, irreversible, since the ultimate constituents of every natural process are actual occasions, subjects of experience that inherit the data for their self-constitution from antecedent occasions and similarly influence their successors within the next generation of occasions as a result of their immanent "choice" or "decision" here and now.[27]

This last point, however, raises a question with respect to the third and last part of Prigogine and Stenger's book. Therein they conclude that "we live in a pluralistic universe in which reversible and irreversible processes coexist, all embedded in the expanding universe."[28] Their principal contention in that final part of the book, to be sure, is that irreversibility likewise plays a role on the atomic and subatomic levels of activity where the principles of classical dynamics have always held sway. But they are clearly reluctant to affirm with Whitehead that all natural processes, no matter how elementary, are irreversible. Their compromise position, as already noted, is to affirm the second law of thermodynamics as a selection principle for the empirical verifiability or nonverifiability of symmetrical probability schemes within classical dynamics.[29] Only that chain of probabilities which moves toward a state of equilibrium in the future can be empirically verified; its mathematical counterpart, namely, the chain of possibilities leading to a state of equilibrium in the past, is logically consistent but empirically nonverifiable. Hence, increasing randomness or the principle of entropy presupposes irreversibility, movement into the future alone. Yet all this takes place within unstable dynamic systems; within stable dynamic systems the laws of classical dynamics still hold.

Here one may suitably make the distinction proposed at the beginning of this chapter: that all systems within nature are irreversible even though individual processes within those same systems may be time-independent and thus apparently reversible. Even in these specialized cases, however, one may raise the question whether time-independence likewise entails time-inversion or time-reversibility. It may only mean that the time-factor in these processes, that is, the rate of change from one moment to the next, is so negligible as safely to be ignored. Thus equations of classical dynamics that are time-independent, that is, contain no reference to the effects of time, can be appropriately applied to a real-life situation that is virtually timeless (though not absolutely so), provided that one takes into account the abstractive character of those same equations in the first place. That is, one must avoid what Whitehead calls the fallacy of misplaced concreteness in which one treats abstractions as if they were more real than the reality they are intended to explain.

An example from Whitehead's analysis of inorganic compounds should make this point clear. Structured societies of inorganic actual occasions (for example, crystals and other mineral formations) are held together in virtue of the category of transmutation. Diversities of detail in the self-constitution of the constituent occasions are ignored in favor of a common element of form that serves as the operative principle for the society as a whole. In that case, there is virtually no difference between successive generations of actual occasions. Since novelty or change can only take place through conceptual prehensions, and since this type of "mental" activity is at an absolute minimum among inorganic actual occasions, there is little or no ontological basis for distinguishing past from future in the time-span of a rock or crystal. Accordingly, the equations of classical dynamics can suitably be applied to the analysis of such physical processes that are at or near perfect equilibrium. For there is little or nothing in the immediate empirical data that would give the lie to the abstractions represented by the equations. Only if one expands the parameters of investigation so as to include more and more of the environment within which the process in question is situated, does it become apparent that this apparently unchanging entity is part of a much broader *system* that is in full process of evolution.

Prigogine and Stengers themselves seem to have this broader picture of reality in mind when they speak at the end of book three of "the time-oriented polarized nature of the universe in which we live."[30] Furthermore, they maintain that "irreversibility is either true on *all* levels or on none. It cannot emerge as if by a miracle, by going from one level to another."[31] Thus they too seem implicitly to endorse the distinction between time-independence and time-inversion. Clearly, there are processes within nature that appear time-independent. But this does not mean that within them time-inversion is really taking place.

With these remarks, I bring to a close both chapter 3 and the first part of this book, which deals with the notion of society as the foundational concept for a contemporary philosophy of nature. After an introductory chapter in which I discussed the possibility of a new world view or cosmology both for philosophers trained in the classical tradition and for those trained in the natural sciences, I set forth in chapter 1 my reasons for thinking that the Whiteheadian category of society, as least as I understand it, is a better foundational concept for such a new worldview than either a repristinated concept of substance or the notion of "natural system" as developed by Ervin Laszlo and other "systems" thinkers. Then in chapter 2 I raised with natural scientists the following issue: whether the ultimate constituents of material reality are themselves matter in some attenuated form or whether they are, in fact, actual occasions, immaterial subjects of experience that are objectified now as wave lengths of energy, now as particulate matter. In that same second chapter I inquired whether societies, both in the technical Whiteheadian sense and in a more common sense understanding of the term, may be conceived as integrated fields of activity for their constituent occasions. My conclusion was that the field concept, above all, with respect to human communities and ecological systems, represented an advance beyond thinking of those same macroscopic realities as somehow analogous to substances and/or physical organisms. Furthermore, what common sense identifies as substances or physical organisms can likewise be interpreted as integrated fields of activity for innumerable submicroscopic subjects of experience if only one is willing to concede with natural scientists that human sense experience is the end product of a highly sophisticated process of abstraction and simplification.

Finally, in the present chapter I tried to show the parallels between the thinking of Ilya Prigogine and Isabelle Stengers on the reality of irreversible processes within nature and the conceptual scheme of Whitehead in the matter of structured societies or highly organized fields of activity. In both cases, that which originates in a localized part of the system or field gradually becomes diffused through the field by reason of a chain-reaction among the component parts (constituent actual occasions). Furthermore, I indicated that, while Prigogine and Stengers leave open the theoretical possibility of reversible processes within nature, the logic of their own argument seems to draw them toward the position espoused by Whitehead: namely, that all processes within nature are time-irreversible. Even those processes that are at or near perfect equilibrium and thus appear to be time-independent are, nevertheless, parts of a more comprehensive system or field of activity that is in full process of evolution.

Much more, of course, could be said both with respect to these same topics and in view of other related topics. But, within the restricted parameters of the present book, it seems appropriate at this time to move on to its second major division, namely, those chapters dealing with the topic of spirit. The focus of attention, accordingly, will shift from natural science to the history of philosophy. No attempt will be made to trace the origin and development of the idea of spirit within Western thought. But I

will be concentrating on that movement within Western philosophical reflection that concerned itself in a special way with the
nature and reality of spirit in a cosmological setting, namely,
German Idealism. Here, too, however, I will consciously limit
myself to two key figures, Schelling and Hegel. In chapter 4, I
will use the philosophy of Schelling to inquire into the reality of
subjective spirit as the power of radical self-constitution. Chapter
5 will deal with Hegel's notion of objective spirit as embodied in
progressively more comprehensive structures or intelligible patterns. Undergirding these forays into the history of philosophy,
of course, will be the neo-Whiteheadian scheme that I have
already elaborated at some length in the first part of this book.

Part Two
Spirit

4

Subjective Spirit: The Power of Radical Self-Determination

During much of his adult life, F. W. J. Schelling was over-shadowed by Hegel, initially his colleague and friend, but later his bitter rival within the world of academe. Schelling, to be sure, gained reputation and acclaim earlier in life with his widely read works in *Naturphilosophie*. But the spectacular success of Hegel's *Phenomenology of Mind* combined with the mixed reviews accorded to Schelling's *Of Human Freedom*, published two years later in 1809, set a pattern of response to their works in the eyes of the reading public that was never really altered during the lifetime of either Hegel or Schelling. Yet Martin Heidegger, in the introduction to his university lectures on *Of Human Freedom* in 1936, referred to Schelling as the most original of the German Idealists and regarded the latter book as his most insightful work.[1] For in this relatively modest work, Schelling grasped more clearly than Hegel or any of his contemporaries the centrality of the notion of freedom for understanding the nature of Being. With this judgment I fully agree, although, as will be evident below, I have reservations about Heidegger's interpretation of freedom in this context. That is, while I agree that freedom is the ground of Being for Schelling, I do not believe that Schelling in his own way anticipated Heidegger's claim of an irreducible ontological difference between Being and beings. In my judgment, Schelling's profound insight into the intrinsic connection between freedom or spontaneity and the ground of Being can only be fully understood and appropriated when one grasps with Whitehead what it means to be a subject of experience, that is, an innate power of radical self-constitution.

In this chapter, accordingly, I will first offer a brief résumé of Heidegger's interpretation of the *Freiheitsschrift* (*Of Human Freedom*) and then offer my counterinterpretation of the text based on what might be called a dynamic principle of balance

(ein dynamisches Gleichgewichtsprinzip). Afterwards, I will indicate how Schelling's line of thought here, at least to some
extent, anticipates Whitehead's key idea that the being of an
entity is inseparable from its "decision" to be this reality rather
than that. Finally, in the concluding part of the chapter, I will
offer some comments on Wolfhart Pannenberg's carefully worked
out distinction between the ego and the self in his recent book,
Anthropology in Theological Perspective. The implicit focus
throughout the chapter, however, will always be the same,
namely, the notion of subjective spirit as the power of radical
self-determination.

At the beginning of his commentary on the Freiheitsschrift,[2]
Heidegger praises Schelling for grasping the problems inherent
in a systematic, genuinely ontological understanding of human
freedom. For philosophers from Plato and Aristotle onward have
sought to comprehend Being in terms of the totality of beings in
their ordered interrelationships. Post-Cartesian thinkers, moreover, added the further distinction that only in and through
carefully constructed "systems" can one be certain that the
beings of common sense experience are indeed grounded in an
ordered totality that is ultimately synonymous with the divine
being. But Schelling was the first to ask whether and to what
extent the experience of human freedom is compatible with the
presuppositions of such an a priori systematic understanding of
reality. The deepest ontological problem, then, is not how to
mediate between nature and spirit, as in earlier philosophical
systems, but rather how to reconcile freedom and necessity, that
is, the experience of being free with the conviction that all things
are grounded in God as the Supreme Being.[3]

The second point made by Heidegger is that Schelling cor-
rectly looked for an insight into this problem by reflecting carefully upon the sentence: God is all. The "is" of that sentence is
not the articulation of a simple identity between two things (that
is, A equals A), but rather the expression of a Ground-Consequent
(Grund-Folge) relationship whereby God is the ground of everything else that exists. The "is," accordingly, implicitly stands for
a process of grounding in which individual entities have the
ground of their existence in God and yet by the same token exist
in their own right as independent actualities.[4] Hence, instead of
pantheism or the doctrine of the immanence of all things in God
being incompatible with belief in human freedom, it rather de-
mands it. For, as Heidegger comments, "God is man; i.e., man as
a free individual is in God, since only what is free can be in God;

everything unfree and anything else insofar as it is unfree is outside of God."[5] On the other hand, if human freedom, as Schelling says, is the power to choose both good and evil,[6] then how is freedom as the power to choose evil grounded in God? With this question, says Heidegger, Schelling concludes his introduction to the philosophical issues at stake here and begins his own systematic exposition of the nature of human freedom.

The third point that Heidegger makes vis-à-vis Schelling's doctrine of human freedom is that "grounding is ungrounded, there is no reason for reason."[7] That is, Heidegger's conclusion, after working through Schelling's exposition of both the possibility and the reality of a primordial free choice for evil, is that there is no reason for this choice except the free act itself, which is represented by Schelling as taking place outside of time and therefore apart from any possible causal influences within creation. The steps in Heidegger's thinking here can be summarized as follows. Following the text of the *Freiheitsschrift* closely, he first notes that the Ground-Consequent relationship not only applies to the relationship between God and creatures, but also to the relationship within God's own self between Ground and Existence. Creatures, including the human being with his or her capacity for evil, thus have their Ground not in God as an Existent, but in God as the Ground of God's own Existence. Hence, out of the divine Ground, that which is not properly God as an Existent, there proceeds not only God's self but also all creatures (especially and above all, human beings as "spirits" like God). Furthermore, if one analyzes closely the inner nature of these two dialectical principles within the divine being, one realizes that, just like the operation of Ground and Existence within human consciousness, Ground within the Godhead is a prerational desire or striving for self-expression. Existence, on the other hand, within the divine consciousness as within human consciousness, is a rational will (*Wille des Verstandes*) that opposes itself to the prerational will of the Ground and thereby paradoxically generates the unity of the divine consciousness, namely, God as Spirit.

Within this frame of reference for understanding the divine being, the possibility and reality of a primal free choice of human beings for evil can be readily explained. In progressively bringing the will of the Ground into subordination to the rational will within the divine consciousness, God effectively brings into existence creatures that bear a closer and closer relationship to God's own self as the divine spirit. Only in human beings, however, is the likeness to God perfectly achieved; that is, within human beings there is a *conscious* subordination of the will of the Ground to the rational will. Yet precisely here is the possibility of a primal choice for evil to be found. For, as the conscious unity of the will of the ground and the rational will, the human being can reverse the relationship between the two, that is, subordinate the rational will to the will of the Ground, and thus constitute herself or himself as the reverse image of the Creator, namely, as evil spirit. The temptation to effect this reversal of the two wills to one another within her or his consciousness arises, to be sure, from the natural desire of the will of the Ground to seek its own satisfaction in independence of the rational will. Yet, says Heidegger, relying upon the text of the *Freiheitsschrift*, the decision is ultimately that of the human being himself or herself.[8] Moreover, it seems to be a decision which is made without prior deliberation as if this were the only possible choice available to the individual. As Heidegger comments: "He who has yet to decide what he wants to do still does not know what he wants to do. He who knows what he wants has already decided."[9]

The fourth and last point that Heidegger makes vis-à-vis Schelling's exposition on the nature of human (and divine) freedom involves his reservations about the entire scheme. He finds himself, namely, opposed to Schelling's attempt to integrate this new understanding of human freedom within an all-embracing rational system. He sees no need, then, as Schelling evidently does in the final pages of the *Freiheitsschrift*, to justify the reality of evil within the world process as the necessary dialectical counterpoint to the ultimate triumph of good. Furthermore, he sees no reason why God (understood as "Absolute Indifference" or simply as "Love") must be represented as the transcendent ground for the dialectical process of grounding within human (and divine) consciousness described above. For in his mind it would be better to admit (1) that, morally speaking, every human free choice is a mixture of good and evil, and (2) that it is, strictly speaking, inconceivable *(unbegreiflich)*.[10]

What is at stake here, of course, is Heidegger's own distinctive approach to the history of Western metaphysics. In his mind, Schelling errs in providing a transcendent ground for the dialectical principles of Ground and Existence in human consciousness because, in effect, this is a reversion on Schelling's part to the presuppositions of classical metaphysics after having set forth a genuinely new paradigm for the understanding of human existence earlier in *Of Human Freedom*.[11] That is, in distinguishing between Ground and Existence within human consciousness, Schelling was getting at the ontological difference between Being and beings well in advance of Heidegger's own efforts in *Being and Time*. The Ground, in other words, grounds the reality of the human being as an Existent, just as Being grounds the existence of beings in Heidegger's phraseology. In both cases, there is no need to look behind or beyond the concrete ground of existence within the individual human being to a transcendent ground in the divine being. For, this is onto-theology, the corruption of genuine ontology, to which the history of Western metaphysics has been prone since Plato and Aristotle. Thereby Being itself is ignored as one seeks the (logical) ground for the existence of finite reality in an infinite Creator God.

In my judgment, however, what Heidegger fails to notice is that the true ground for the unity of human consciousness in Schelling's philosophy is not the Ground as the dialectical principle opposed to Existence; nor is it the Ground of the divine being. Rather, it is the inscrutable act of free choice whereby the individual human being determines the relationship between the two principles in human consciousness and thus becomes "spirit," either a good spirit in imitation of God as the divine spirit or an evil spirit in an at least implicit rebellion against God. In either case, the ground of human existence is not a dialectical principle but a free choice or, more precisely, the *power* of free choice, which is constantly being exercised in order to confirm or change the order existing between the Ground and Existence within human consciousness. In support of this contention, however, it will be necessary to clarify what I mean by a dynamic principle of balance *(ein dynamisches Gleichgewichtsprinzip)* as the implicit paradigm for the exercise of both divine and human freedom in *Of Human Freedom*.

Some years ago, in an article entitled "Gleichgewicht als Seinsprinzip: Schellings Philosophie des Gleichgewichts," the well-known Schelling scholar Hermann Zeltner conjectured that one of the basic paradigms operative in Schelling's philosophy was a dynamic principle of balance.[12] That is, given the omnipresence of dialectically opposed principles in his thought, one should realize that the duality of principles always arises out of an antecedent unity and exists only to bring into being another form of unity on a still higher level of existence and activity. Accordingly, while the originating unity is presumably undifferentiated, that is, logically antecedent to the division into conflicting principles of activity, the subsequent unity is differentiated. For it exists only in and through the interaction of the two dialectically opposed principles. In my own study of the nature of divine and human freedom in Schelling's philosophy,[13] I used this paradigm to conclude that for Schelling the individual human being is initially the undifferentiated unity out of which two dialectical principles within her or his consciousness arise: namely, the will of the Ground and the will to Existence. Eventually, one of these two principles is subordinated to the other and thereby a new differentiated unity of consciousness is created, which Schelling calls "personality" (Persönlichkeit) or "spirit" (Geist).[14] It is the individual human being, however, as the underlying subject of the process, who ultimately makes the decision with respect to which principle will be superior to the other. Thus the human being by this decision effectively constitutes her or his new self-consciousness as personality or spirit.[15]

In response to this scheme, one might well object that for Schelling the decision whereby a human being becomes personality or spirit is not a conscious one; it is a choice that seems already to have been made as soon as one begins to reflect upon it. This would seem to be the reason, moreover, why Heidegger sees an irreducible dualism between Ground and Existence in Schelling's philosophy.[16] The Ground is constantly giving rise to Existence as its dialectical opposite; thus, no conscious free choice is present because none is needed. But, thought through to its ultimate consequences, such an argument seems to deny the reality of freedom altogether. Freedom no longer has anything to do with decision or choice but simply is the result or outcome of a dialectical process between rival principles in human consciousness.

There is, however, still another alternative, namely, that the choice or decision is preconscious, that is, that it is actually made before one becomes conscious of it. As I will indicate below in the final section of this chapter, the human ego as the power of radical self-constitution is not aware of itself as exercising that power but only of the self that it already is in virtue of that power. Consciousness, after all, has to do with what is objective, namely, what is already fixed and determined; it cannot, accordingly, be aware of what is still becoming and thus undetermined. Put in other terms, the decision that effects the unity of consciousness cannot itself be part of consciousness.

What Kant called "the original synthetic unity of appercep-tion,"[17] therefore, is the result, not of a primitive decision that is made at the beginning of time or outside of time, as Schelling presents it in *Of Human Freedom*,[18] but rather of a decision that is made over and over again in time, but at a preconscious level. Moreover, this constantly repeated decision presupposes the on-tological capacity or power to make such a radically self-con-stituting decision. This, I would argue, is human subjectivity as such: namely, the originating, still undifferentiated unity of con-sciousness or *Abgrund*, which in Schelling's scheme precedes the opposition of Ground and Existence within divine (and human) consciousness.[19]

My thinking here is heavily conditioned by Whitehead's doc-trine of actual occasions as momentary subjects of experience constituted by a immanent preconscious "decision." For the mo-ment, however, I only wish to make clear that the text of the *Freiheitschrift* basically supports this interpretation. For, as Zeltner points out, Schelling was fascinated by the idea of du-ality arising out of a primordial undifferentiated unity and issu-ing into a differentiated unity of opposites in dynamic interrelation. Furthermore, Schelling laid great stress on the fact that a decision is required to overturn the priority of the rational will over the will of the Ground and that presumably another decision (or series of decisions) is needed to restore the proper order between the two principles in human consciousness. All that I am suggesting is that Schelling's fanciful appeal to a deci-sion made outside of the realm of space and time is unnecessary. It can be much more easily explained as a constantly repeated preconscious decision whereby the dialectical oppositions within human consciousness are resolved one way or another. As Schelling himself says, human freedom is "the power of good *and* evil."[20] Hence, the individual continually has to take a stand with respect to competing principles within his or her con-sciousness in order to preserve psychological integrity. For this reason, the individual will either take the same stance as in the previous moment or alter it slightly. But in either case, he or she will become conscious of that decision only after it is made. For, as Heidegger perceptively comments, "He who knows what he wants has already decided."[21]

After completing *Of Human Freedom*, Schelling continued to reflect on the dynamics of human and divine freedom in subse-quent lectures and manuscripts. In the Stuttgart lectures of 1810, for example, he first conjectures that there are in human nature two principles, the one conscious and the other unconscious, and that the process of human self-development (der Prozess unserer Selbstbildung) consists in lifting the unconscious principle gradually into consciousness. He then continues: "From that moment in which we become aware of the two principles within us, make a division within ourselves, set ourselves against ourselves, lift the better part of ourselves over the lower part, from that moment on consciousness begins, but for that same reason not yet full consciousness."[22] Then in the uncompleted Weltalter (Ages of the World) manuscripts, Schelling notes that an inner dialogue between Past and Present within human consciousness can only take place if the individual is prepared constantly to separate the two by an act of free choice. "The human being who cannot make a division within himself, cannot liberate himself from all that has happened to him and actively oppose himself to it, has no Past or, better, never comes out of it, lives constantly within it."[23]

On the basis of these and similar passages in the Weltalter manuscripts, Wolfgang Wieland concludes: "Freedom as a foundational structure for being human is the ground for the possibility, either to create a distinctive Present or to remain caught in an undifferentiated Past."[24] A few pages later, after having analyzed Schelling's concept of the Future as a basic openness to further self-determination, Wieland remarks: " As one who separates himself from himself, a human being understands himself not as the subject who accomplishes this separation, but as the very act of separation itself. Thus the state of separation and the act of separation are experienced as a single reality within temporal consciousness."[25] Wieland, it should be noted, was consciously employing the insights of Heidegger into the temporality of human existence (as expressed in Being and Time and other writings) so as to systematize Schelling's somewhat scattered reflections on the nature of time in the Weltalter manuscripts. In Being and Time, for example, Heidegger proposed that the path to authentic human existence lies in "resolve" (Entschluss), existential self-determination.[26] Then, in Kant and the Problem of Metaphysics, he probed into the Kantian "transcendental imagination" (transzendentale Einbildungskraft) and concluded that it really should be named "transcendence" (Transcendenz), that is, the power of human subjectivity to project a "world" in which Being would be present as the implicit horizon for the conceptual understanding of all concrete objects of experience.[27] Finally, in Vom Wesen des Grundes, he proposed that the deeper meaning of *Transcendenz* is freedom: not the freedom of an individual free action *(Willensakt)*, but the freedom that is constitutive of *Transzendenz* itself.[28] Thus freedom is the ground of the ground of Being.[29]

Quite consistently with Heidegger's principles, therefore, Wieland laid heavy stress on freedom as the root of human subjectivity in his studies of temporality in Schelling's *Weltalter* writings. He concluded, first of all, that for Schelling of the *Weltalter* period a human being being experiences the passage of time only insofar as he grounds it in a radical decision separating past from present.[30] Furthermore, this free act has to be constantly repeated in order to maintain the unity of temporal consciousness as the dialectical interplay of past, present, and future.[31] Finally, Wieland also perceived that the very selfhood of the human being is grounded in this decision; that is, the individual is not first a subject who then makes such a decision, but rather the individual becomes a subject precisely in making the decision.[32]

Why, then, did Wieland not move logically from the self-constituting free decision to an underlying power of decision-making as its ontological source or ground? At least two reasons may be proposed. First, following the lead of his intellectual mentor, Heidegger, Wieland may have been wary of a regression therewith to *Willensmetaphysik*, the traditional understanding of the human subject as the enduring substrate for the intentional activities of knowing and willing.[33] Because he lacked, in other words, an explicit process understanding of reality such as Whitehead sets forth in *Process and Reality*, Wieland could not think in terms of a power of radical self-determination without reverting to substance-oriented ways of thinking. Hence, he focused simply on the act of existential free choice and solved the question of its ontological source or ground in terms of the dialectical interplay between Ground and Existence within human consciousness. Yet this would seem to be more of a nominal than a real solution for the metaphysical issue at stake here, since it is not at all clear how dialectical principles within consciousness can simultaneously function as the ontological ground for the very existence of consciousness in the first place.

Secondly, Wieland seems to have followed Heidegger in maintaining that the Ground-Existence relationship in Schelling's thought is an anticipation or foreshadowing of Heidegger's own key insight into the ontological difference between Being and beings. Hence, to appeal to something like the *Gleichgewichts-*

prinzip whereby the dialectical opposition between Ground and Existence is itself grounded in a primordial undifferentiated unity would seem to deny the validity of the ontological difference between Being and beings. Is this, however, necessarily the case? Whitehead, for example, proposes in his philosophy that every actual entity (including God as the primordial actual entity) is what it is in virtue of its own self-constituting decision. But he also holds that it has this power of radical self-determination only by reason of participation in Creativity, the motive force for the world process as a whole. Creativity, moreover, is not itself an entity, but rather the principle of the world process that exists in all its instantiations, although in none of them exclusively. Hence, even God as the primordial actual entity is "a creature transcended by the creativity which it qualifies."[34] Accordingly, if one is willing to identify Being in Heidegger's philosophy with Creativity in Whitehead's scheme, then it is possible simultaneously to maintain the ontological difference between Being and beings (that is, between Creativity and the entities in which it is instantiated), and to hold that any given entity (God included) is grounded in its own subjectivity, that is, its immanent power of radical self-determination.

Furthermore, given the fact that the process of concrescence for an actual entity consists in an appropriate blend of physical and conceptual prehensions, something like a dynamic principle of balance *(Gleichgewichtsprinzip)* is at work in its self-constitution. The duality of physical and conceptual prehensions is overcome in the higher synthesis that is achieved in the entity's self-constituting decision. Likewise, physical prehensions (like Schelling's will of the Ground) represent raw feelings that need to be ordered and shaped prior to the amount of decision by conceptual prehensions (for Schelling, the rational will). The parallels here should not be overdrawn since Whitehead was not nearly so committed to dialectical thought-patterns as Schelling was. But both men were careful students of human nature who, as I see it, were convinced that (human) subjectivity basically consists in the power of radical self-determination. Moreover, quite apart from Schelling's admittedly ambivalent position on this matter, Whitehead was clearly no advocate of *Willensmetaphysik*; that is, he did not suggest that the actual entity is in any sense an ontological substrate for a subsequent decision as to its self-constitution. Rather, it exists as a subject only in virtue of the decision-making process and ceases to exist as soon as the decision is made. This presupposes, of course, that the conscious subject of common sense human experience is not a single enduring reality but instead a temporally ordered series of momentary subjects of experience (what Whitehead calls "a personally ordered society of actual occasions"). But the key metaphysical issue here is that for Whitehead (and, I believe, for Schelling also, although less clearly so) human subjectivity is grounded, not in God as First Cause of all else that exists nor in some dialectical principle within human consciousness such as the will of the Ground, but in its own power of radical self-constitution.

In the third and final part of this chapter, I wish to review and further reflect upon the distinction between the ego and the self that Wolfhart Pannenberg proposes in his recently published *Anthropology in Theological Perspective*. With customary thoroughness, Pannenberg digests the results of the research of many different individuals on this subject before setting forth his own position. He makes reference, for example, to the North American philosophers William James and George Herbert Mead, to Continental thinkers like Martin Buber, Franz Rosenzweig, Jean Paul Sartre and Martin Heidegger, and finally to Sigmund Freud and Erik Erikson as psychologists who have done seminal work in this field. Interesting for our purposes in this chapter, however, is his suggestion that the earliest attempt to think through the unity of the ego and the self should be traced to Schelling's predecessor in the movement of German Idealism, Johann Gottlieb Fichte.[35]

In the original edition of the *Wissenschaftslehre* (1794), Fichte set forth as the first and unconditional principle of a science of knowledge the hypothesis that the ego posits itself in being.[36] This raises the question, however, whether the empirical ego known in self-consciousness is identical with the "absolute" ego that produced self-consciousness through its act of self-positing. As Pannenberg comments, Fichte seems eventually to have realized the nonidentity of the empirical ego with the absolute ego and to have grounded the reality of the absolute ego in God and God's activity of self-revelation.[37] While Hegel and subsequent thinkers were critical of this facile transit from philosophy to theology, their own efforts to conceive self-consciousness as a process of mediation whereby the self is progressively appropriated through knowledge of the object of knowledge, the nonself, likewise proved to be a failure. For, such a totally objectified self is clearly not identical with the ontological subject of the process of mediation, the ego in its primordial reality as a self-positing activity.

Pannenberg's own solution to the problem of the unity between the ego and the self is heavily dependent upon the theory of William James that the unity of consciousness is due to the synthesizing activity of the ego from moment to moment, albeit in heavy dependence upon the self (both social and individual) out of which it is continuously emerging. Thus, in opposition to Fichte, he says:

> The ego is not the continuously existing subject of my individual development, a subject that is always present behind all changes in consciousness and gives ever new definitions of itself in the process of its identity formation, but is not itself changed thereby. Rather, the ego is primarily tied to the moment and receives its continuity and identity only in the mirror of the individual's developing consciousness of itself as the totality of its "states, qualities, and actions."[38]

In my judgment, Pannenberg is exactly correct on this point. The ego or the momentary subject of experience is basically a power of synthesis issuing in a decision that ends the process of self-constitution for this moment, however brief. Yet the ego can only synthesize what is given to it by the self: that is, previous mental states, sensations or other bodily feelings, and, finally, the external world as mediated through the sense organs of the body. The ego, in other words, experiences both its identity with its past self and, in some vague way, its distinctness from that same self in that it is a new and different moment in the overall process of self-constitution. It is free to become itself within the limits imposed by its own past history.

My only reservation with Pannenberg's position here has to do with whether the ego as distinct from the self is self-conscious, i.e., aware of its own synthesizing or decision-making activity. Siding with Whitehead, I would argue that the ego (understood as a concrescing actual occasion) is not, strictly speaking, self-conscious. The self of which it is conscious is the self of the immediately preceding moment from which it is here and now distinguishing itself. It cannot simultaneously be aware of its own identity if only because that identity is not yet determined or complete. Only its successor in the sequence of occasions constituting the self will be conscious of what it de facto became. "No actual entity can be conscious of its own satisfaction [the termination of its process of concrescence]; for such knowledge would be a component in the process, and would thereby alter the satisfaction."[39] Hence, the ego is only indirectly self-conscious, that is, through its linkage with and derivation from the self. Pannenberg seems to be making much the same point when he comments: "Only indirectly, insofar as the 'I' of the isolated moment is known as identical with 'myself,' and therefore as the momentarily present manifestation of that totality of states, qualities, and actions that in the eyes of a 'generalized other' are to be ascribed to the individual which I am—only in this way does the 'I' as such acquire a continuity that lasts beyond the isolated moment."[40] Yet it remains ambiguous whether for Pannenberg the 'I' in this passage is self-conscious, that is, aware of its own synthesizing activity and thus aware of its own identity, however momentary, in distinction from the self.[41]

In the same chapter of his book, however, Pannenberg introduces a new concept, namely, that of person, which helps to clarify his position on the complex relationship between the ego and the self. "Person," he says, "is the presence of the self in the moment of the ego, in the claim laid upon the ego by our true self, and in the anticipatory consciousness of our identity."[42] Thus understood, personhood has temporal thickness. It exists, to be sure, from moment to moment in the ego as the power of radial self-determination. But, insofar as it is the presence of the self in the moment of the ego, it represents the past as well as the present. Finally, since in Pannenberg's words it is an anticipation of the individual's complete identity, it likewise includes the future. Person, therefore, rather than ego, would seem to be the appropriate term to describe the common-sense experience of self-consciousness in which one feels oneself existing in the present but at the same time emerging out of the past and tending toward an as yet undefined future.

Furthermore, at least as I interpret it, Whitehead's analysis of temporal consciousness as a personally ordered society of actual occasions yields the same results. That is, each constituent actual occasion is a dynamic synthesis of past, present, and future with the necessary consequence that the personally ordered society itself exhibits both temporal thickness and a developmental teleology. To be more specific, each occasion is a dynamic synthesis of past, present, and future because as a concrescing subject of human experience it recapitulates "with peculiar completeness"[43] its predecessors in the same society, and as a superject it thrusts its now determinate actuality upon its successors.[44] But, if this is true of each member of the society, then the society as a whole must possess, as noted above, both temporal thickness and a developmental teleology. For succeeding one another without interruption in this way, the individual occasions constitute a persistent pattern of order or intelligibility within the society (understood as the *field* of temporal consciousness[45]). This pattern, to be sure, is not fixed or predetermined after the fashion of an Aristotelian entelechy or final cause. Rather, it represents simply a teleological orientation, a directionality with respect to the anticipated future. For otherwise the individual human being would not be a person with a definite character or personality.[46]

If, then, Whitehead's analysis of human consciousness as a personally ordered society of actual occasions is basically compatible with Pannenberg's notion of person, there is all the more reason to think of the ego in his scheme as comparable to a Whiteheadian actual occasion. It is a power of radical self-constitution that has to be exercised anew at every instant in order to sustain the unity of temporal consciousness. It is, moreover, both conscious and unconscious. It is conscious of its linkage with the self, that which it already has become. But it is unconscious of what it here and now is becoming through its own immanent "decision."

But, one may ask, why is it so important that the ego in its self-constituting activity be unconscious or, more precisely, preconscious. The reason, quite simply, is that one then does not confuse subjective spirit or subjectivity with consciousness. As noted at the beginning of this chapter and repeated at regular intervals thereafter, subjective spirit is fundamentally the power of radical self-constitution. In some (but by no means all) entities, the exercise of this power results in consciousness or, in the case of human beings, self-consciousness. But spirit as an immanent capacity for self-determination is likewise operative within actual occasions constitutive of inanimate realities such as rocks and crystals. Similarly, it is the ontological principle within actual occasions making up plants and lower-level animal organisms lacking in consciousness. Hence, contrary to what might be considered a major presupposition of modern Western philosophy, spirit and consciousness are not synonymous. A measure of spirit is to be found in every actual occasion and in every society to which it belongs, whether that society be the reality of an atom or the reality of a highly complex animal organism such as a human being. The full significance of this proposal about the nature of subjective spirit, however, will be evident only after we have worked through the implications of objective spirit in the next chapter.

5

Objective Spirit: Structured Fields of Activity

Hegel's doctrine of objective spirit is perhaps the clearest and most persuasive section of his philosophy. It is certainly the one in which he has made best use of his wide observations of men and events.[1]

While concurring with James Collins in this estimate of the wide-ranging influence of Hegel's reflections on right, morality, and ethical life, I will not focus in this chapter on the details of the latter's moral and political philosophy. Rather, my attention will be directed to the underlying notion of objective spirit as such, that which comes into actuality (Wirklichkeit) as a result of the exercise of human rights by morally responsible individuals within the context of family, civil society, and the state. My contention, in brief, is that objective spirit for Hegel is the realm of intersubjectivity insofar as the latter is incarnated in progressively more comprehensive and structured fields of activity between human beings as (at least implicit) members of a social whole or society.

As such, Hegel's notion of objective spirit bears a distinct resemblance to what I have set forth in this book as a Whiteheadian (or neo-Whiteheadian) notion of society, that is, the spatio-temporal field for the interrelatedness of actual occasions in virtue of a common element of form. Hegel, to be sure, limits the realm of intersubjectivity to human beings as finite conscious spirits. But, as I mentioned at the end of the last chapter, this is to equate subjectivity with consciousness, indeed, with self-consciousness. Whitehead's argument, on the other hand, is that all actual occasions, even those constitutive of subatomic particles, are subjects of experience. Hence, their spatio-temporal interrelatedness within a given field of activity is an instance of intersubjectivity on a more fundamental level of existence and activity. Human intersubjectivity is thus the climax of pro-

gressively more complex levels of intersubjectivity, beginning
with the conjunction of subatomic energy-events to form first
atoms, then molecules, cells, and entire organisms.

Should the notion of objective spirit be expanded, therefore,
beyond what Hegel explicitly envisioned so as to include the
world of nature? To answer this question properly, it will be
necessary to study more carefully the generic idea of spirit in
Hegel's philosophy and to review what I have already set forth
about the category of society in Whitehead's thought. From a
comparison and contrast of these two pivotal concepts, it should
become clear that, while they represent two different solutions to
the perennial philosophical problem of the One and the Many,
they nevertheless both presuppose the same metaphysical principle, namely, that the whole is greater than the sum of its parts.
Hence, they both set forth what might be called an organismic or
idealistic approach to reality, as opposed to a mechanistic or
materialistic understanding that would assert that the whole is
nothing more than the sum of its parts. The chapter, accordingly,
will be divided into two parts. In the first part, I will compare
and contrast the rival concepts of spirit and society. Then, in the
second part, I will show how both concepts, properly understood, illuminate what I myself mean by objective spirit as progressively more comprehensive and structured fields of activity
for a quasi-infinite number of subjects of experience.

Before contrasting spirit in Hegel's philosophy with society in
Whitehead's scheme of things, however, I think it advisable to
explain my understanding of the relationship of spirit to two
other Hegelian categories, namely the Concept (Begriff) and the
Idea. As I see it, Absolute Spirit is the full self-realization or
actuality (Wirklichkeit) of the Idea in and through the power of
the Concept.[2] If what is true of Absolute Spirit is likewise true of
spirit in its finite manifestations, then it seems clear that spirit,
wherever it exists, is a more or less adequate self-realization of
the Idea through the power of the Concept. Further generalizing
from this, I would argue that the three categories are related to
one another as follows: spirit is primarily an actuality, the Concept is primarily an activity, and the Idea is its immanent telos or
orientation.

Admittedly, one could urge that both the Idea and the Concept
are more real (or actual) than spirit since the Idea is realized
through the power of the Concept in the realm of logic and the
world of nature before being realized in the sphere of activity
proper to spirit. But the realization of the Idea in the realm of

logic is in the sphere of ideality, not reality; that is, it simply represents the dialectical ordering of concepts with respect to the Idea itself as the immanent goal or *telos* of the movement of thought. Furthermore, the realization of the Idea in the world of nature signifies the presence of spirit at a preconscious level. Hegel himself speaks of the Idea at this stage of development as "mind implicit, slumbering in Nature."[3] My own contention would be that spirit in some form or other is present in nature wherever there exists a totality in which the whole is more than the sum of its parts. The Idea, in other words, is the unity of the real and the ideal that is achieved in some inanimate reality or, even more so, in some natural organism through the activity of the Concept insofar as the latter is the principle of self-organization for the entity in question. But the consequent interplay of parts with the whole and vice versa is mute testimony to the presence of spirit, albeit in an inchoative form. The very fact that the material entity is a totality, that is, a dynamic unity of functioning parts or members rather than a simple aggregate or heap of separate entities, indicates that the material elements have been lifted into an organic unity. They no longer represent pure "externality" but, taken together, some limited degree of "internality" or self-organization, the unerring sign of the reality of spirit.

A brief overview of the ground plan of Hegel's *Philosophy of Nature* should make my point clear. Section one, titled "Mechanics," deals, first of all, with space and time. Both space and time represent Nature's self-externality. Space as "wholly ideal side-by-sideness"[4] is the positive expression of that self-externality; time as the ongoing sublation of the subsistence of space is its negative expression. Space and time, says Hegel, continually pass over into one another and the identity of that which thus moves is matter.[5] Matter itself, however, is particularized into bodies that are held together as a system or totality by the force of gravity. In rapid strokes, therefore, Hegel sketches the movement from the pure self-externality of nature in space and time to the concept of the solar system as a totality, a dynamic unity of interdependent parts or members that thus exhibits the reality of the Idea in the world of mechanics. I would only add that even at this level of existence and activity spirit is inchoatively present wherever material entities (for example, planets) are gathered together into a functioning totality. As Hegel notes in his introduction to the *Philosophy of Nature*, "Nature is in its own self this process of becoming Spirit, of sublating its otherness."[6] But, if it is indeed the process of becoming Spirit, nature is in some real sense already spirit whenever a new totality comes into being.

Basically the same principles govern Hegel's discussion of physical and chemical processes in the second part of the *Philosophy of Nature*. The earth, for example, is not only one of the four primitive elements (along with air, fire, and water) but also "the totality which holds together the different moments [elements] in individual unity, . . . the power which kindles them into a process which it also sustains."[7] Yet earth itself is differentiated into physical bodies with varying characteristics. These, in turn, are reunited with one another in virtue of electrical and chemical processes that exhibit once again the logical form of a totality or dynamic union of opposites. In the third and final part of the book, "Organics," Hegel deals initially with "the inanimate organism of the earth," which, subsequent to its own process of formation in terms of the above-mentioned physical and chemical processes, continually gives birth to rudimentary, purely transient forms of life: "lichens, infusoria, and in the sea countless hosts of phosphorescent points of life."[8] This is succeeded by a discussion of plant life in which the parts of the organism are imperfectly distinguished from one another and thus in some measure interchangeable with one another. In animal life, on the other hand, the various parts of the body are much more fully integrated with one another, and the organism as a whole enjoys a certain individuality vis-à-vis its peers. But even here, at least on a prehuman level, the individual exists for the species rather than vice versa. Hegel's point in this entire discussion thus seems to be that spirit is latent everywhere in nature and that, given the proper circumstances, it manifests itself in terms of progressively more organized and self-sufficient organic totalities.

Hegel, of course, confined the sphere of *conscious* spirit to human beings, both in their individual psychological makeup and in their interactions with one another within the family, civil society and the state. But, as noted above, given the ultimate identification of spirit, the Concept and Idea in the actuality of Absolute Spirit, it seems appropriate to suggest that spirit is *unconsciously* present wherever nature succeeds in organizing itself into a totality or dynamic unity of functioning parts or members. Spirit, in other words, is synonymous with actualities (as in Absolute Spirit), whereas the Concept and the Idea are metaphysical principles through which the actuality in question comes into being and is sustained in existence. Furthermore, given this identification of spirit with the actuality of a totality (or organized field of activity) wherever it is to be found, some very illuminating comparisons can be made with the Whiteheadian notion of society.

As noted earlier, spirit in Hegel's philosophy and society in Whitehead's scheme of things represent different solutions to the perennial philosophical problem of the One and the Many even though they both presuppose that the whole is greater than the sum of the parts. To deal with the latter point first, Hegel's whole philosophy is based on the premise that truth and being exist, first and foremost, in the totality and only in the parts or members insofar as they are integrated into the totality. His comment in the preface (Vorrede) to the Phenomenology of Mind is illuminating here, "The Truth is the whole, but the whole only insofar as its nature (Wesen) is mediated through a process of self-development."[9] Furthermore, Hegel's key distinction between concrete and abstract universals rests on the presupposition that the actuality proper to the whole (the concrete individual) is greater than the actuality proper to the parts or members (the various abstract universals that signify one or other dimension of the reality in question).[10]

Whitehead's comments on the nature of a society are equally instructive. "The point of a 'society,' as the term is here used, is that is it self-sustaining; in other words, that it is its own reason. Thus a society is more than a set of entities to which the same class-name applies: that is to say, it involves more than a merely mathematical conception of 'order.' "[11] Whitehead goes on to say that the common element of form is present in each member of the society "by reason of genetic derivation from other members of that same society," a point which I will discuss more fully below. The key idea here, however, is that a Whiteheadian society as a patterned field of activity is in some sense an actuality in its own right. As Whitehead comments, it is its own reason; it is self-sustaining. Accordingly, it is an ontological totality, that is, a structured whole that is more than the sum of its constituent actual occasions.

As already mentioned in chapter 1, this is a controversial point among Whiteheadians. Many, citing Whitehead's remark at the beginning of Process and Reality that actual entities "are the final real things of which the world is made up,"[12] contend that the only ontological unity possible within a Whiteheadian universe is the subjective unity of the individual actual entity, its process of unifying the data available to it in order to become itself. Yet,

without the objective unities of the various societies to which
individual actual entities belong, Whitehead's philosophy is unquestionably a form of metaphysical atomism. Furthermore if
Whitehead's philosophy is atomistic, then, as Wolfhart Pannenberg comments, it paradoxically repeats "the style of thinking
characteristic of materialism, the very thing to which Whitehead
wanted to offer an alternative."[13] That is, even though its "atoms"
or ultimate constituents of reality are subjects of experience
rather than inert particles of matter, it follows the same reduc-
tionistic approach to reality as classical materialism. For, as
noted earlier, the dividing line between an organismic/idealistic
and a mechanistic/materialistic approach to reality does not lie
so much in the nature of the ultimate constituents of reality, but
rather in the positive or negative attitude taken toward the metaphysical principle that the whole is greater than the sum of its
parts. Idealists hold that the principle is true, hence, that there
exist objectively intelligible unities within nature that synthesize
the "atoms" or ultimate constituents according to various dynamic patterns or configurations. Materialists, on the other hand,
reject this principle, arguing that every apparent whole or ontological totality is reductively nothing more than the sustained
interaction of its constituent parts.

There is, to be sure, a very real sense in which, as Whitehead
notes, "the ultimate metaphysical truth is atomism."[14] But this
only means that there are ultimate constituents of reality, that
every whole or functioning totality is analyzable into constituent
parts or members. Furthermore, as I shall indicate momentarily,
the objective unity of the whole may well emerge out of the
dynamic interaction of its constituent parts or members rather
than possess a predetermined structure or form of intelligibility.
But the crucial issue here is that, however they originate, there
exist synthetic wholes objectively intelligible to the human
mind, that they are not reductively "class-names," as Whitehead
would say, for aggregates of entities with only analogous relationships to one another. Despite some ambiguity of terminology,
therefore, Whitehead would seem to be in the idealist camp on
this point; his basic notion of a society as something that is its
own reason and is thus self-sustaining carries with it the further
implication that it possesses an objective unity that is reflected in
the self-constitution of its constituent actual occasions.

At the same time, Whitehead's notion of society is not the same
as Hegel's understanding of spirit. While they agree that the
whole is more than the sum of its parts, they disagree on the way

in which the form and the material elements interact in order to produce the whole in question. For Hegel, in line with the philosophy of Plato, Aristotle, and the entire classical tradition, the form communicates its preexistent unity to the disparate material elements in order to shape them into an organized whole. The close interconnection between the Idea, the Concept, and spirit is thereby confirmed, since at any given level of existence and activity in nature spirit represents the more or less successful incarnation or embodiment of the Idea in the conditions of matter through the immanent activity of the Concept. What is important for Hegel, therefore, is the progressive self-realization of the Idea in various ontological totalities up to and including Absolute Spirit, its perfect form of expression. For Whitehead, on the other hand, the form is derived moment by moment from the genetic interrelatedness of the actual occasions making up a given society (or structured field of activity). At least in principle, the form is thus never exactly the same from moment to moment since it is the byproduct of successive generations of actual occasions in dynamic interrelation.

Here one might well object that Whitehead is a materialist in his thinking, after all. That is, for him the whole is nothing more than the sum of its parts since by their dynamic interrelation they produce the whole from moment to moment. This would seem, however, to be an instance of the genetic fallacy, that is, a confusion of the nature and function of an entity with its manner of origin. Simply because the common element of form governing a given society arises out of the individual self-constitution of its member actual occasions does not mean that it fails to perform its own proper function, namely, to provide a basis of unity for the society or structured field of activity at that instant and to be an object of conceptual prehension for the next generation of occasions that will make up the society or field of the next instant. It is, in other words, functioning as the form of the ontological totality very much like the substantial form within Aristotelian metaphysics, even though its character or specific intelligibility at any given moment is intrinsically dependent upon the concomitant interrelatedness of its material elements. Thus, while clearly not a materialist, Whitehead shows more sensitivity than Hegel, Aristotle, or other philosophers of the classical tradition to the strict interdependence of form and matter. At every instant the form originates out of the interrelatedness of the material elements; but for that same instant it is the reason why they are this reality rather than another, or, even more fundamentally, why they are an ontological totality rather than a simple aggregate of separate entities in spatial juxtaposition.

At this juncture I am ready to set forth my own understanding of objective spirit. As should be apparent from my analysis of the Hegelian notion of spirit and the Whiteheadian category of society, it will inevitably present a synthesis of these two pivotal concepts, a mediating position between what Hegel and Whitehead explicitly had in mind with spirit and society respectively. From Hegel's notion of spirit, I draw the idea that ontological totalities are more than aggregates of material elements by reason of an immanent principle of self-organization that unites these elements to one another and constitutes them an intelligible whole or structured field of activity. From Whitehead's understanding of society, I derive a twofold insight. First, the "material elements" are not matter in the traditional sense; that is, they are actual occasions, momentary subjects of experience that by their dynamic interrelation produce the effect of materiality on the human senses. Secondly, by their dynamic interrelation, these occasions co-produce the common element of form, the objective intelligibility, which gives them their unity as a society or structured field of activity for that particular instant. Unlike the Idea in Hegel's philosophy, therefore, the common element of form in Whitehead's scheme does not preexist its incarnation in a given field. Rather, it comes into being with the actual occasions themselves as the concrete form of their interrelatedness within the field.

Whitehead, to be sure, likewise talks about "eternal objects" as entities with a timeless reality. But the "complex eternal object" that is the common element of form for a society at any given moment is in a very real sense unique to that society; as noted above, it is the concrete form of relatedness for precisely these (and not some other) actual occasions.[15] In this passage, Whitehead also talks about the analogous "feelings" that the occasions possess in virtue of their inheritance of the same common element of form. This, too, indicates that the complex eternal object is a singular rather than a strictly universal reality since feelings are invariably rooted in the subjectivity of the occasions in question and thus are only partially communicable. At the same time, of course, in its cognitive dimensions the common element of form is sufficiently communicable from one generation of occasions to the next so as to guarantee the ongoing perpetuity and stability of the society as a whole.

Objective spirit, then, is the realm of intersubjectivity insofar as the latter is incarnated in progressively more comprehensive and structured fields of activity for momentary subjects of experience. Whereas objective spirit is limited to the realm of human intersubjectivity in Hegel's philosophy, I follow Whitehead in introducing subjectivity into the world of inanimate nature, indeed, into the ultimate constituents of reality. Hence, any ontological totality within Hegel's philosophy of nature is, in terms of this hypothesis, an instance of objective spirit since it represents at any given moment a structured field of activity for a given number of actual occasions. These occasions, moreover, as already noted in the preceding chapter, exhibit the reality of subjective spirit by reason of their immanent power of radical self-constitution. They are thus individual instances of subjective spirit that collectively by their dynamic interrelation produce the structured fields of activity proper to objective spirit. There is, accordingly, a deeper continuity between the world of nature and the world of the spirit or the world of intersubjectivity than Hegel himself seems to have envisioned. For both subjective and objective spirit are already at work in the world of nature below the level of conscious self-awareness. The actual occasions constitutive of an atom, for example, are not aware of themselves as interrelated subjects of experience. But they nevertheless behave as such when through the process of their individual self-constitution they co-constitute the structured field of activity known to us humans as an atom. An atom, then, is an instance of objective spirit in the world of nature.

In chapter 3, where the connection between Whiteheadian structured societies and dissipative structures in chemistry and biology was analyzed, I indicated how Whitehead accounts, first for the appearance of life, then for the emergence of consciousness within the world of nature. Hence, while he does attribute a primitive form of "mentality" to the actual occasions constitutive of atoms and molecules in that they must prehend both physical data and conceptual patterns from the world of their predecessors as part of their own process of self-constitution, he does not suggest that these same inorganic occasions are living, still less, that they are conscious. Living actual occasions are, so to speak, a new "grade" of occasion that comes into existence only at the level of structured societies when the various subsocieties of inorganic occasions have reached a sufficiently complex level of interrelationship. Similarly, life gives rise to conscious life only when the network of living occasions is sufficiently dense that it can support "a thread of personal order along some historical route of its members,"[16] in other words, when it can sustain a soul, animal or human. Finally, Whitehead recognizes a fourth "grade" of actual occasion, specific to human self-consciousness, in which critical judgment is added to imaginative enjoyment for the enrichment of experience.[17] Thus, like Hegel, Whitehead makes distinctions between nonlife, life, and rational life. But, unlike Hegel, he introduces subjectivity, understood as the power of radical self-constitution, into the ultimate constituents of reality so that form and/or structure, wherever it appears, is already the work of objective spirit in the sense explained above.

At the same time, Hegel's expansive vision of progressively more complex ontological totalities in the realm of human intersubjectivity (that is, the movement from family through civil society to the structured reality of the ideal state) contrasts sharply with the relatively sparse remarks made by Whitehead in *Adventures of Ideas* and elsewhere on the structure and proper functioning of human communities, both civil and religious. While the generic concept of structured society, for example, should in principle apply to human communities as well as to physical organisms, it is apparent that the functioning of a community cannot simply be likened to the functioning of a physical organism without grave danger of collectivism or totalitarianism within the body politic. The soul, as we have already seen in chapter 3, exercises agency for the entire physical organism; but there is no subsociety within the body politic corresponding to the soul. For Hegel, on the other hand, the relationship between the individual citizen and the state is very carefully specified. Is there any way, then, in which Hegel's reflections in the area of political philosophy can be used to compensate for the relatively undeveloped character of Whitehead's thoughts on the same subject?

Before answering this question, I should summarize briefly Hegel's notion of the state as set forth, above all, in his *Philosophy of Right* and compare it with Whitehead's more informal treatment of the state and civil society in *Adventures of Ideas*. The state, says Hegel, "is the self-conscious ethical substance, the unification of the family principle with that of civil society."[18] That is, whereas in a family the feeling of love uniting all to one another tends to prevail over the otherwise legitimate needs and aspirations of individual members, the opposite state of affairs reigns in civil society. That is, the members tend consciously or unconsciously to use one another for the satisfaction of their personal needs and to pay little or no attention to the notion of the common good. The state, accordingly, is "the actuality of the ethical Idea,"[19] because it combines the emphasis on the common good resident in the family with the enjoyment of personal independence characteristic of life in civil society. The state as an ontological totality, in other words, subsists in the activity of its citizens vis-à-vis one another; it has no existence apart from that same activity. But the citizens, in turn, are thereby obligated to make their individual good identical with the common good. They must live for the state and its interests if the state is to subsist in them as its citizens.[20]

At the same time, different individuals perform different functions within the state. The king, for example, represents the reality of the state in his own person and as such is the ultimate decision-maker within the body politic.[21] But in this decision-making he is assisted both by government officials and by members of the two legislative assemblies, the one representing the landed aristocracy and the other the commercial class. The ultimate sovereign power within the state, however, resides not in any individual or group of individuals, but in the constitution, which as the objective expression of the rational idea of the state controls the lives of all of them.[22] As Hegel comments, "In a well-organized monarchy, the objective aspect belongs to law alone, and the monarch's part is merely to set to the law the subjective 'I will.' "[23] But the law itself as proposed by the legislative assemblies should be a legitimate development or further particularization of the true idea of the state as contained in the constitution.[24]

Like Hegel, Whitehead too believes that the various subgroups within a given society "should contribute to the complex pattern of community life, each in virtue of its own peculiarity. In this way individuality gains the effectiveness which issues from coordination, and freedom obtains power necessary for its perfection."[25] But, unlike Hegel, Whitehead anticipates that these "Professions," for the most part, will be unconcerned about the general purposes of the state as they pursue what they regard as their own best interests. Hence, compulsion in some form or other will have to be exercised by government officials in order to bring them into effective harmony with one another. Whitehead is not espousing here a highly individualistic "laissez-faire" approach to civil society since he explicitly repudiates the social-contract theories of government prevalent in seventeenth and eighteenth century Europe.[26] Rather, in contrast to Hegel, he seems to regard strife to be just as important as harmony in the gradual evolution of political structures:

> If you side with Francis Bacon and concentrate on the efficient causes, you can interpret large features of the growth of structure in terms of "strife". If, with Plato, you fix attention on the end, rationally worthy, you can interpret large features in terms of "harmony". But until some outline of understanding has been reached which elucidates the interfusion of strife and harmony, the intellectual driving force of successive generations will sway uneasily between the two.[27]

From a structural point of view, the differences between Hegel and Whitehead on this point would seem to reduce to the fact that for Hegel the state is a single organism, albeit with many interrelated parts, and for Whitehead it is a structured society or complex field of activity for its citizens. Accordingly, for Hegel harmony must be the key value since an organism cannot long survive when its members are in serious competition with one another. For Whitehead, on the contrary, strife or at least competition can play an equally significant role within the state since the latter is seen as the social environment or field of activity for the ongoing interaction of individuals and subgroups with one another. As David Hall comments, Whitehead occupies an intermediate position here between organic theories of the state such as Hegel proposed and the purely analytical approach to the state, which is found in the social-contract theories of Thomas Hobbes and John Locke. Thus "he is able to provide, in the phylogenetic discussion of the types of order, the concept of a non-living structured society which is only a partial analogue of the living structured society comprising the human mind-body complex."[28]

At this point, we are already involved in an implicit evaluation of Hegel's and Whitehead's political philosophy. Hence, I will state my own position on this matter as succinctly as possible. As I see it, the two approaches to political life have rival strengths and weaknesses, so that each in some sense needs the other in order to guard against the bias inherent in its own position. The strength of Hegel's understanding of the state, for example, is the focus on the unity of the social organism, its reality as an ontological totality distinct, in some measure at least, from the activity of the citizens simply regarded as individuals. The corresponding weakness of this approach, of course, is the tendency toward totalitarianism, above all, in view of the fact that a single individual, namely, the king, ultimately makes all decisions affecting the group. The fact that the king himself is accountable to the provisions of the constitution is only a partial safeguard against the danger of dictatorship since Hegel allows for "development" in the interpretation of the constitution over a period of time. Thus, under the rubric of developing what is explicitly stated in the constitutions, the king could effectively exercise despotic control over his subjects. In the case of a weak-willed king, of course, the same despotic power would be inevitably exercised by that subgroup within the state to whom the king felt most obligated.[29]

Contrarily, the strength of Whitehead's understanding of political life is that it explicitly allows for the unity of the state to arise out of the sometimes competitive, sometimes harmonious interplay of groups with one another and, indeed, of individuals with one another within each of these same groups. This, of course, is an extension or further application of Whitehead's basic premise in *Process and Reality* that "agency belongs exclusively to actual occasions."[30] Naturally, a human being is not a single actual occasion. Rather, the soul of a human being is a temporally ordered society of actual occasions that coordinates and directs the structured society that is the total human organism. *A fortiori*, subsocieties within the state are not actual occasions but instead even broader structured societies or fields of activity that exist in virtue of the interrelated agencies of their human members. Whitehead's basic point, however, is upon reflection quite clear. Agency belongs exclusively to actual occasions in the sense that only occasions make decisions with respect to their intrinsic self-constitution; they alone are subjects of experience in the strict sense. Societies of various sizes come into being as a result of the interrelated character of the decisions of individual actual occasions. Societies, accordingly, do not make decisions with regard to their structure or self-constitution; hence, they do not exercise agency in the strict sense reserved for the activity of actual occasions.

Yet, as already mentioned in chapter 1, Whitehead seems to have overlooked the possibility of a corporate agency proper to societies, which arises out of the interrelated character of the individual agencies of the constituent actual occasions of the society in question. It is, therefore, not an agency that issues from a single decision, as in the case of an actual occasion, but one that flows out of a series of decisions. With respect to a personally ordered society such as the human soul, for example, it is a temporally ordered series of decisions that effects the ongoing agency of the soul and, through the soul, of the entire human organism from moment to moment. In the case of a highly complex structured society such as one of the "Professions" described by Whitehead in *Adventures of Ideas*, it is both a spatially and temporally ordered series of decisions that constitutes the corporate agency of the group. That is, human beings spatially distinct from one another have to work together over a sufficiently lengthy period of time to achieve a genuine sense of corporate identity and effectively to pursue common goals and values.

Thus the weakness of Whitehead's political philosophy, as I see it, is that he does not have an adequate theoretical foundation to account for the agency of various groups within the state in their ongoing interaction and for the agency of the state as a whole in dealing with other states in the field of international politics. To say that the agency of these corporate bodies reduces to the agency of their constituent members is questionable since it seems to imply a form of atomism in the area of political philosophy. Here, in my judgment, is where Hegel's doctrine of objective spirit offers a valuable corrective to Whitehead's reflections on political life. Above all in his understanding of the state as the synthesis of family life and civil society, Hegel is quite clearly maintaining that agency belongs not simply to individuals, but to corporate bodies as well. As already noted, there are genuine dangers to this organismic approach to political life. But there is an equally grave danger in reducing the activity of political bodies simply to the interaction of individual human beings with one another. Thus, as mentioned earlier, the differing approaches of Hegel and Whitehead to political philosophy are truly compensatory since each position in a very real sense needs the other to guard against the bias inherent in its own perspective.

To sum up, then, in this chapter I have developed a notion of objective spirit that is partly of Hegelian and partly of Whiteheadian inspiration. In effect, I have compared and contrasted the Hegelian notion of spirit with the Whiteheadian category of society. As a result, I was able in the first part of the chapter to suggest that objective spirit is present in nature wherever the material elements are organized into a functioning ontological totality or structured field of activity through the unifying power of the Concept. Since objective spirit is a matter of form or structure, there is no need for the totality itself to be conscious, still less, self-conscious as with human beings. All that is required is that the form or structure of the field come into being through the interaction of subjects of experience with one another. Here, of course, is where Whitehead's notion of society as the dynamic interrelatedness of actual occasions (subjects of experience) in virtue of a common element of form proved invaluable for expanding Hegel's notion of objective spirit into the realm of subhuman nature. Upon close inspection, the material elements themselves are composed of immaterial subjects of experience that by their dynamic interrelation paradoxically produce the impression of inert matter upon the human senses. Thus the ontological totalities to which Hegel refers in his *Philosophy of Nature* are already, in Whiteheadian terms, structured societies, that is, fields of activity whose constituent members are subjects of experience or actual occasions. Spirit, accordingly, both subjective (interrelated subjects of experience) and objective (the resultant structured field of activity for their interrelatedness) is unquestionably present in subhuman nature at a preconscious level of existence and activity.

Afterward, in the second half of the chapter, I initially compared and contrasted Hegel's and Whitehead's separate approaches to political philosophy. Once again, I found that only a synthesis of the two views provided the balance needed for a deeper understanding of the role of objective spirit in the realm of human intersubjectivity. That is, Hegel's notion of the state and other institutional bodies as agencies of corporate activity in some sense distinct from the individual agencies of their constituent members has to be balanced off against Whitehead's insight into the state as a structured society, that is, a patterned field of activity for groups that are sometimes in conflict, sometimes at peace, with one another. Objective spirit, therefore, is not the self-expression of a suprahuman individual subjectivity, as Hegel seems to have imagined, but rather the ongoing self-expression of a complex community of individual subjectivities. But this latter topic, namely, the possibility and reality of an all-embracing community of "spirits," will be discussed in part three of this book, dealing with the God-world relationship.

Part Three
Society and Spirit

6

The Triune God

Thus far, I have tried to make clear what I understand by society and spirit taken separately. In this third and last part of the book, I will combine the two ideas in order to present a new understanding of the God-world relationship. I will try, in other words, to show how subjective spirit, understood as the power of radical self-determination, and objective spirit or society, understood as a structured field of activity for entities endowed with subjective spirit, can be combined to produce a model for a genuinely panentheistic understanding of the God-world relationship. Panentheism, it will be remembered, maintains that, while all finite entities exist in God and through the power of God, they are ontologically distinct from God in terms of both their being and activity.[1]

Given the notion of substance as the first category of being within classical metaphysics, it has always been difficult to conceive the God-world relationship in panentheistic terms without ultimately identifying the world with God or God with the world. Even in the process-relational metaphysical schemes of Whitehead and Hartshorne, where one might expect a consistent panentheistic approach to the God-world relationship, difficulties are present, as I shall indicate below. Yet, using the notions of society and spirit developed in the preceding chapters, I hope to present a genuinely panentheistic understanding of the God-world relationship. For, if larger fields by definition contain smaller fields that are still governed by their own laws or patterns of activity, it should be possible to reconceive the God-world relationship in terms of interrelated fields of activity within which the three divine persons and all their creatures continuously come into being and are related to one another.

In the present chapter, accordingly, I will focus primarily on the antecedent understanding of God required for such a field-oriented approach to the God-world relationship. In the next chapter, I will spell out in greater detail the implications of this theory for the understanding of Ultimate Reality as a cosmic society, which includes both God and all finite entities. My major resource in the present chapter will be my own earlier published work, *The Triune Symbol: Persons, Process and Community*, since, as I see it, only an understanding of God as a community of three divine persons allows one to speak of the nature of God as an all-encompassing field of activity within which creation finds its "place." Within the philosophical schemes of Whitehead and Hartshorne, on the other hand, where God is conceived in uni-personal terms, a field-oriented approach to the God-world relationship is much more problematic.

To begin, then, I will first summarize my understanding of God as a community of divine persons in *The Triune Symbol* and then show how it can be modified to conform to the notion of Whiteheadian societies as structured fields of activity developed in the present text. While implicitly agreeing with Charles Hartshorne that God should be understood as a personally ordered society of actual occasions rather than as a single, ever-concrescing actual entity (as Whitehead himself proposes), I argued in this earlier text that each of the three divine persons should be understood as a personally ordered society of occasions and that their unity as one God is the unity of a Whiteheadian structured society or society of subsocieties.[2] My reasoning was basically the same as that presented in chapter 1 of the present manuscript, namely, that through the interrelated agencies of its constituent occasions from moment to moment, a society possesses an objective unity sufficient to sustain its structure and/or character from moment to moment. Hence, the three divine persons co-constitute from moment to moment their communal reality as one God through their interrelated activities vis-à-vis one another.

These activities I then spelled out in the following manner. At every instant God the "Father"[3] proposes to the divine "Son" a possibility for their co-existence as a community of divine persons. The "Son" in that same instant responds invariably (but still freely) to the proposal of the "Father" with an unequivocal yes. The third person of the Trinity, the divine Spirit, is simultaneously active in this dialogue between the "Father" and the "Son," prompting the "Father" to offer and the "Son" to respond. As a result, their continued coexistence as a community is necessarily dependent upon the ongoing cooperation of all three divine persons. The "Father" alone cannot actualize the possibilities for their common existence that the "Father" offers to the "Son." The "Son," on the other hand, can only actualize what the "Father" concomitantly offers by way of possibility. Finally, the Spirit is indispensable to sustain the dialogue between the "Father" and the "Son" but is dependent upon their ongoing exchange for the Spirit's own existence as a member of the divine community.[4]

Admittedly, this is only a model, not a picture, of the inner life of the three divine persons. As already mentioned in my introduction, a model is merely a symbolic representation of aspects of reality that are not directly accessible to us. What it attempts to describe is ultimately a mystery; but the mystery (here, the God-world relationship) may well be illuminated by carefully thinking through the logical consequences of the model. Thus, as I see it, the invariant relationship between "Father," "Son," and Spirit described above explains how human beings and indeed all finite entities, without loss to their own individual identity, participate in the communitarian life of the three divine persons. To be specific, in *The Triune Symbol* I reserved to the "Father" what Whitehead simply ascribes to God: that is, the transmission of divine initial aims to each new generation of finite occasions so as to initiate their respective individual processes of concrescence. It was appropriate that the "Father" should take on this function with respect to creatures since within the model given above it is the "Father" who offers the equivalent of a divine initial aim to the "Son" in the power of the Spirit at every instant. Very much in line with traditional trinitarian theology, therefore, the "Father" is then the source of life not only for the divine "Son," but for all creatures; as stated in the Nicene Creed, the "Father" is the "Maker" of heaven and earth.

Similarly, it is fitting that the "Son" should be associated with the human race and indeed with all of creation as its focal point or head. For, within the model proposed above, it is the "Son" who responds to the offer of the "Father" at every moment. The "Son," accordingly, can and should be the focal point of the response of all finite occasions, both individually and collectively, to the offer of the "Father" in their respective processes of concrescence. The initial aim of the "Father," in other words, is in one respect the same for all finite occasions, namely, that they should join their limited and invariably somewhat conditional response to the "Father's" initial aim for them to the unlimited and unconditional response of the divine "Son" to the "Father." Only in this way is a unified world achieved from moment to moment. That is, whereas Whitehead claimed in *Process and*

Reality that the multiplicity of individual occasions is unified from moment to moment within the "consequent nature" of God,[5] I proposed in *The Triune Symbol* that the multiplicity of finite occasions at any given moment constitutes a cosmic society under the headship of the "Son" in the "Son's" ongoing response to the "Father."[6] The created universe, therefore, is at every instant both a semiautonomous reality governed by its own laws and patterns of activity and, in virtue of its ordination to the "Son" in the "Son's" ongoing response to the "Father," a participant in the communitarian life of the three divine persons, the ultimate society.[7]

Finally, because the Holy Spirit is the mediating principle between the "Father" and the "Son" within the above-mentioned model, it is only natural that the Spirit should play a similar role in the relation of creation as a whole and each finite occasion in particular to the "Father" and the "Son." That is, in line with this theory, the Spirit prompts the "Father" to continue offering initial aims at every moment to each new set of concrescing occasions and prompts those same occasions to unite their response to the "Father's" initial aims with the ongoing response of the "Son" to the "Father." In this way, the Spirit acts as the creative and vivifying principle within all of creation and, above all, within the minds and hearts of human beings, even as the Spirit is the effective vivifying principle within the Godhead.

All these reflections I summed up in the following diagram (cf. figure 1). Imagine three circles in the overall shape of a triangle: two at the base and one above and between the other two. The one at the base on the left-hand side should be designated as the "Father"; the one at the base on the right-hand side, the "Son"; and the one above and between the other two, the Spirit. Further, imagine within the circle at the base on the right-hand side two other concentric circles, one within the other. The larger one represents creation as a totality; the smaller one, the human community. The human community is thus the key process within the overall process of creation, but creation as a whole is part of the inner life of the divine "Son" in the "Son's" ongoing response to the "Father" through the power of the Spirit.

As I indicated at the time, the problem with this diagram is that one is thereby led to imagine that the three divine persons are distinct individuals who are just extrinsically joined to one another in a loose association. Hence, instead of being represented as three circles spatially distinct from one another, they should rather be conceived as a single sphere with three different

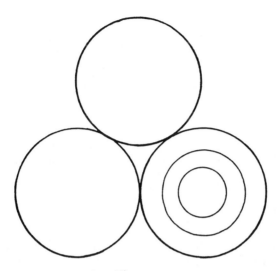

Figure 1

dimensions (that is, height, width, and depth) to correspond to the reality of three persons who are collectively one God. Yet, at the time, it was difficult for me to imagine how creation and the human race could thus be pictured as focused on the "Son," if the "Son" had no particular place within the all-encompassing sphere of the divine life. Here, in effect, I was encountering some of the inevitable limitations of a model derived from material reality to describe what is basically a psychic or spiritual reality. That is, Whiteheadian actual entities (both infinite and finite) encompass all of reality in their self-constitution and thus perfectly interpenetrate without losing their own standpoint or identity.[8] But how is one to represent that in a two-dimensional diagram?

One further point should be mentioned before bringing this summary of my presentation of the God-world relationship in *The Triune Symbol* to a close. Whitehead describes Creativity in *Process and Reality* as "that ultimate principle by which the many, which are the universe disjunctively, become the one actual occasion, which is the universe conjunctively."[9] As such, Creativity is a metaphysical "given," since even God is in this respect a "creature" of Creativity, requiring the power of Creativity for the divine self-constitution.[10] In virtue of my trinitarian understanding of God, I was able, on the contrary, to propose that Creativity is the underlying nature of God, that is, the power of divine intersubjectivity whereby the three divine persons at every moment come into existence and are related to one another as an all-embracing structured society.[11] My reasoning ran as follows. While I agreed with Whitehead that Creativity is the power for the subjective unification of actual occasions, I further argued that it must logically also be the power whereby these same occasions are integrated into societies of various kinds at every moment.

> What binds individual actual entities into a society is a "common element of form" which is part of the internal self-constitution of each member entity. In empowering each individual occasion to become itself, creativity likewise provides that it prehends the common element of form characteristic of the universe as a whole from a moment ago and that same common element of form as further specified for all the various subsocieties to which the occasion belongs. Hence, simply by becoming itself according to a certain pattern, the individual occasion simultaneously becomes a member of a myriad number of hierarchically ordered societies up to and including the world process as a mega-society of societies.[12]

If one applies this line of thought to each of the divine persons understood as a succession of actual occasions and to their objective unity as one God in the form of a Whiteheadian structured society, then it is easy to see how Creativity may be termed the power of divine intersubjectivity. For, in virtue of Creativity, each of the divine persons is constituted at every moment both as an individual entity and as a member of a structured society, namely, the divine community. The reality of the one is inseparable from the reality of the other. The divine community only exists in virtue of the self-constituting activity of the persons at every moment, and the persons in their self-constitution are shaped by the common element of form proper to their existence as a divine community.

Furthermore, in line with this same understanding of Creativity as the power of divine intersubjectivity, I also suggested that the "Father's" initial aim to creatures at every moment is not simply a directionality for the exercise of their share in the power of Creativity, but likewise the communication to them of this selfsame power of Creativity (understood as belonging to the divine persons by nature). "The individual [finite] entity, in other words, comes into being through its own decision, . . . but only because the Father gives it a share in the divine being, i.e., the power of intersubjectivity whereby it exists simultaneously in itself and in relation to others."[13] In this way, I was able to reaffirm from a process-oriented perspective traditional Christian belief in God the "Father" as Creator of heaven and earth even as I safeguarded what seemed to be the essential point of Whitehead's own doctrine here, namely, that all actual entities, finite and infinite alike, come into being in virtue of a radical power of self-constitution communicated to them at the beginning of their concrescence. Likewise, I gave new emphasis to Whitehead's own insistence on the social character of reality. For not only are actual entities interrelated because each is the microcosm of the universe.[14] They are also interrelated because in virtue of Creativity they constitute societies of various kinds up to and including the all-embracing society or community of the three divine persons.

In any event, I will now attempt to rethink this basic scheme in terms of my key insight of the present book, namely, that Whiteheadian societies are structured fields of activity for their constituent actual occasions. Put in the simplest terms, this would mean that each of the divine persons is a subsistent field of (intentional) activity and that their ongoing interaction with one another results in a common field of intentional activity, which I would identify as the extensive continuum within Whitehead's categoreal scheme. Each of the elements in this statement, however, requires further explanation. First of all, each of the divine persons is a subsistent field of intentional activity. As noted earlier, I implicitly follow the lead of Charles Hartshorne in suggesting that God is not a single ever-concrescing actual entity as Whitehead suggested, but rather a society of actual occasions. I differ from Hartshorne in supposing that God is not unipersonal but tripersonal. Hence, each of the divine persons is a society of occasions. Furthermore, since divine occasions like finite occasions are necessarily transient realities or momentary occurrences, the enduring reality of each of the divine persons is a society or, as I would propose, a structured field of intentional activity. The field, to be sure, never exists apart from its constituent occasion of the moment; but what endures is the field, not the occasion.

Whitehead, as noted earlier, conceived God as a nontemporal, ever-concrescing actual entity.[15] Perhaps what he implicitly had in mind with the notion of God as an ever-expanding reality was the image of a field controlled by a divine Mind that keeps adjusting each successive addition to the field or each new phase of divine development to all its predecessors. If so, then this is quite close to what I propose for each of the divine persons. Each of them is a series of divine occasions with infinitely broad scope and intensity of experience. Each divine occasion prehends its predecessors "with peculiar completeness"[16] in and through their objectifications in the field. There is then a succession of occasions but no sense of temporal passage between occasions since each incorporates the effects of the decisions of all its predecessors into its own self-constituting decision and feels therewith the full subjectivity of its predecessors within its own subjectivity. Equivalently, therefore, each of the divine persons is like a continuously existing divine Mind with an infinite number of phases of development.

Yet, if each of these divine persons is an intentional field of *infinite* scope and duration, then, logically their fields must coincide and thus produce a single common field of intentional activity. Furthermore, within this common field, each of the divine persons prehends at every moment not only the objectifications of its own past occasions but also the objectifications of the past occasions of the other two divine persons. The only difference between them is that each prehends its own subjectivity differently from the way in which it prehends the subjectivity of the other two persons. That is, in prehending the objectifications of its own past occasions within the common field, each divine person identifies with the subjectivities therein represented more completely than it does with the subjectivities of the other two persons as represented by their objectifications in the common field of activity. Thus each of the divine persons fully understands the subjectivity of the other two persons without totally identifying with it. Likewise, each of the divine persons retains its own subjective identity within the field of intentional activity common to them all, which is their reality as one God.

I also proposed above that this unbounded field of intentional activity for the three divine persons is to be identified with the extensive continuum within Whitehead's categoreal scheme. Admittedly, for Whitehead the extensive continuum is, like Creativity, simply a metaphysical "given." It is the "relational complex in which all potential objectifications find their niche. It underlies the whole world, past, present, and future."[17] It is broader than the space-time continuum proper to our own cosmic epoch since it is not restricted by the patterns of order already established within the latter.[18] Yet, for these same reasons, it seems appropriate that the extensive continuum co-constitute with Creativity the underlying nature of the triune God. As Jorge Nobo argues, the extensive continuum "is that eternal factor of the universe *wherein* the creative advance of actuality occurs."[19] But, as I have argued above, if the enduring reality of God is an unbounded intentional field of activity for the three divine persons, then, this field seems to coincide with the extensive continuum.

On the one hand, it provides the "receptacle" for all the progressive actualizations of the three divine persons with respect to one another and their creatures; it is also a receptacle for all the actualizations of finite occasions as they take place in the space-time continuum and share in the divine communitarian life in the manner indicated above. On the other hand, as a field of intentional activity for the three divine persons, it is not limited to the past and present of the space-time continuum but extends into the future of our cosmic epoch as well; likewise, it includes other cosmic epochs that may have already come into being or will someday come into being; finally, it includes worlds that will presumably never come into actuality but that remain as pure possibilities for the divine persons within their common understanding of the divine primordial nature. Linked as it is with the eternal and unchanging character of the divine primordial vision of possibilities, the extensive continuum is thus eternal and unchanging. Though involved in the becoming of every actual occasion (both finite and infinite), it does not itself become since it is simply the *wherein* of all becoming.

Earlier I stated that the extensive continuum and Creativity together co-constitute the divine nature. Jorge Nobo links them together as distinguishable, but inseparable, aspects of the ultimate ground of the organic universe: "Insofar as this ground is the whereby of all becoming, it is termed 'creativity'; and insofar as it is the wherein of all interconnected actual existence, it is termed 'extension.'"[20] My argument would be that they are indeed distinguishable but inseparable dimensions of the ultimate ground of the universe, but that this ground is the underlying nature of the triune God. For, along with their creatures, the divine persons come into existence at every moment within the extensive continuum in virtue of the principle of Creativity, as noted above. Hence, the extensive continuum and Creativity co-constitute first the ground of their own divine being and then by extension or participation the ground of all created entities as well. Presumably, Nobo himself did not make this inference because, in fidelity to Whitehead's own scheme, he thought of God in unipersonal rather than trinitarian terms. Hence, the extensive continuum and Creativity must be metaphysical "givens," ontologically independent both of God and of creatures. Only if one thinks of God as a community of three divine persons who share a common field of intentional activity and who co-exist as members of this community in virtue of the principle of Creativity, do the extensive continuum and Creativity cease to be independent "givens" and become part of the divine nature, that which is constitutive of the actuality of God from moment to moment.

Elsewhere in his book, Nabo argues that the ultimate metaphysical ground of the universe must also be an "envisioning reality" so that it can create the "dative phase" of each new actual occasion as it begins its concrescence.[21] Without entering into a discussion of Nobo's hypothesis about the "dative phase" of finite occasions here, I would only point out how curious it is that Creativity as an impersonal principle of becoming may be said to "envision" anything. Admittedly, Whitehead himself in *Science and the Modern World* referred to the "underlying activity" as engaged in three types of envisagement: "first, the envisagement of eternal objects; secondly, the envisagement of possibilities of value in respect to the synthesis of eternal objects; and lastly, the envisagement of the actual matter of fact which must enter into the total situation which is achievable by the addition of the future."[22] But this only makes clear the awkwardness of separating Creativity from God (or, more precisely, from the underlying nature of God) within Whitehead's own scheme. Whitehead, to be sure, wanted to avoid a simple equation of Creativity with God, since that would make God ultimately responsible for all the evil in the world as well for what is good.[23] But, if he had conceived God in trinitarian terms as a primordial society of divine persons quite apart from creation, then, he could have identified Creativity with the underlying nature of God that is consistently employed for good rather than evil by the divine persons in virtue of their ongoing self-constituting decisions.

Furthermore, instead of positing Creativity as the intermediary between God and the world,[24] he could have stated, as I have argued above, that the "Father" communicates a share in Creativity (understood as the underlying divine nature) to each new finite occasion with the divine initial aim. For, likewise here, Creativity is simply an impersonal principle of becoming, which must be exercised for good rather than evil by the decisions of concrescing occasions. In the case of finite occasions, of course, it is not certain that Creativity will be employed for good rather than evil. But, in any event, Creativity in itself is neither good nor evil; it can, therefore, without moral ambiguity be regarded as constitutive of the divine being.

One further point needs to be clarified before I conclude this exposition of the nature of God in terms of Creativity and the extensive continuum. In *The Triune Symbol* I argued that all three divine persons share in the divine primordial nature and in the divine consequent nature:

> Thus all three persons prehend the same eternal objects within their common primordial nature, and all three persons prehend as part of their common consequent nature whatever happens in creation. They prehend these contingent events, to be sure, as happening primarily to the Son in whom creation has its being and to the other two persons in virtue of their shared existence with him. But all three are equally affected by whatever happens in creation.[25]

Since they are three subjectivities co-constituting one objective reality, no other explanation of these key terms within a trinitarian framework seems possible.

The "Father," to be sure, is associated in a special way with the common primordial nature since it is the function of the "Father" to propose "initial aims" derived from the primordial nature for the response of the "Son" and of all creatures at every moment. Likewise, as noted above, the "Son" is associated in a special way with the divine consequent nature since it is the "Son" who is the focal point of the response to the "Father" by the "Son himself" and by all creation. Finally, if only for the sake of symmetry, one might argue that the Holy Spirit is to be associated with the so-called superjective nature of God, which Whitehead describes in *Process and Reality* as "the character of the pragmatic value of his specific satisfaction qualifying the transcendent creativity in the various temporal instances."[26] Because the Holy Spirit is viewed as prompting the "Father" to offer initial aims and the "Son" and all creatures to respond to those same promptings, the Spirit seems in a special way to be associated with the mediating activity of Creativity both within the divine community and in creation. The Spirit, in other words, appears to be the hypostatized Superject of the ongoing relationship between the "Father" as representing pure potentiality and the "Son" together with all creatures as representing actuality here and now. Yet, granted all this, the basic point remains the same: namely, that the three divine persons are one God, not three gods;

hence, they all share, at least in some measure, in the divine primordial nature, the divine consequent nature and the divine superjective nature.

What adjustments can and should be made in this scheme, however, given the further hypothesis that the underlying "nature" of God is co-constituted by Creativity and the extensive continuum? Is there still another understanding of "nature" at work here that has to be reconciled with the above-stated three-fold nature of God as primordial, consequent, and superjective? Given the fact that the space-time continuum represents an actu-alization of the extensive continuum and that Creativity is operative in the concrescence of actual occasions which fill out the space-time continuum at every moment, it would seem that one can appropriate to different divine persons various features of this other scheme as well. The "Father," for example, can be associated in a special way with the field of possibilities that constitutes the extensive continuum. For, as noted above, it is the "Father" who chooses at every moment a new set of initial aims for the "Son" and all creatures. Likewise, the "Son" may be associated in a special way with the space-time continuum since the latter is a partial actualization of the full reality of the "Son" within the divine community. Finally, the Spirit, as in the pre-vious scheme, may be appropriately associated with Creativity as the dynamic principle whereby at every moment the extensive continuum is being actualized or concretized in terms of the relations between entities in the space-time continuum.

Yet, just as in the earlier scheme, one must be careful not to destroy the unity of the divine being by distinguishing too sharply the different roles played by the divine persons. All three divine persons through their intentional activity pervade the entire field of the extensive continuum. All three divine persons are affected by events taking place within the space-time con-tinuum. Finally, all three persons are at every moment energized by the principle of Creativity both to be themselves, to constitute the divine community, and to aggregate to themselves all the finite occasions brought into existence in that same moment. Hence, they co-constitute the objective unity of a single struc-tured society or divine field of activity, albeit with multiple dimensions, at every moment.

In the next chapter, I will consider more in detail how finite occasions are continually joined to the divine community so as to constitute an ever-growing cosmic society that is Ultimate Reality within this scheme. But, to bring this chapter on the concept of God to a close, I would like briefly to compare my understanding of God as developed here with the concept of God set forth first by Whitehead and then by his most celebrated disciple, Charles Hartshorne. For, as I see it, my understanding of God deserves the attention of Whiteheadians and other students of process-oriented modes of thought, if only because it seems better than the other two to solve the difficulties connected with the notion of panentheism, that is, the belief that creatures exist both in themselves and in God at the same time.

As noted earlier, Whitehead sees God and the world as "the contrasted opposites in terms of which Creativity achieves its supreme task of transforming disjoined multiplicity, with its diversities in opposition, into concrescent unity, with its diversities in contrast."[27] Hence, there is no doubt that Whitehead thought of the world as ontologically independent of God even as it exists in a dialectical relationship with God. But one must not forget that the world in terms of its constituent occasions is never the same from moment to moment. Our senses, to be sure, give us the picture of the world as an unchanging material reality. But this is illusory; all that really endures are the orderly patterns created by successive generations of momentary occasions. These patterns, I have argued, provide the structure for a myriad number of interlocking fields of activity that from moment to moment constitute the created universe. But, quite apart from that, it seems safe to say that, while the world as such survives, its components are continually perishing.

Precisely to guard against this supreme evil of "perpetual perishing,"[28] Whitehead stipulated that in and through the divine consequent nature God saves "the world as it passes into the immediacy of his own life."[29] But, in thus solving the problem of "perpetual perishing," Whitehead inadvertently created another. For within his scheme, God alone survives. The world as distinct from God "survives" only in a qualified sense, namely, as a totality whose components are never the same from moment to moment. In any deeper sense, the world survives only through incorporation into the divine being. Seen from this perspective, the entire raison d'être of the world is to provide an ongoing increment to the actuality of God. In *Process and Reality*, Whitehead refers to time as "the moving image of eternity."[30] More precisely, the entire space-time continuum should be referred to as "the advancing edge of eternity." It survives only as part of the actuality of God which is itself an actualization of the extensive continuum.

Whitehead's doctrine on God is certainly not pantheistic since it does provide for the ontological independence of the world as an ever-changing totality from God. But it is likewise not a form of panentheism either. For, in the end, only God survives. Finite entities are incorporated into God as soon as they acquire determinate being in the created order; hence, they never exist independently of God, as a strict doctrine of panentheism would seem to require. Likewise, even in the brief interval of their individual processes of concrescence, they do not constitute a world or cosmos in the strict sense. As Whitehead clearly implies in *Process and Reality*, finite occasions acquire their solidarity with one another only in God:

> There are thus four creative phases in which the universe accomplishes its actuality. There is first the phase of conceptual origination, deficient in actuality, but infinite in its adjustment of valuation. Secondly, there is the temporal phase of physical origination, with its multiplicity of actualities. In this phase, full actuality is attained; but there is deficiency in the solidarity of individuals with each other. . . . Thirdly, there is the phase of perfected actuality, in which the many are one everlastingly, without the qualification of any loss either of individual identity or of completeness of unity. . . . In the fourth phase, the creative action completes itself. For the perfected actuality passes back into the temporal world, and qualifies this world so that each temporal actuality includes it as an immediate fact of relevant experience.[31]

In the second phase, accordingly, finite occasions achieve actuality in relative isolation from one another. They first become an ordered totality or cosmos in the third phase, that is, within the consequent nature of God where they are everlastingly one, without loss of individual identity or completeness of unity.

Given this evident deficiency in Whitehead's understanding of the ontological independence of the world from God, is my own theory of the God-world relationship as outlined in this chapter any more successful? I believe that it is more successful for two reasons, though discussion of one of these reasons will have to be postponed until the next chapter. For in the next chapter I will propose that finite occasions retain their subjective immediacy even after their incorporation into the communitarian life of the three divine persons. In this way, Ultimate Reality is not simply the reality of God, but the reality of a cosmic society in which the divine persons share their communitarian life with all their creatures. Details of this scheme must wait for now.

The second reason, however, arises out of the hypothesis of the present chapter, namely, that the three divine persons co-constitute a shared field of activity that includes within it the field of activity proper to creation. The notion of a field, in other words, which can include within itself subfields of activity without damage to the relative autonomy or mode of operation of the subfields, is my response to the speculative dilemma posed by the doctrine of panentheism, namely, how human beings and other creatures can exist both in themselves and in God at the same time. To be specific, by their self-constituting decisions at every moment, the divine persons have a direct influence on the field of activity proper to creation since the latter is part of their own field of activity. As noted above, finite occasions respond to the initial aims of the "Father" in union with the "Son" through the power of the Spirit. Thus a trinitarian structure pervades the world of creation without being directly perceptible by human beings. Similarly, finite occasions by their self-constituting decisions both structure the world of creation and add richness and depth to the communitarian life of the three divine persons. That is, their collective response to the "Father" enriches the response of the "Son" to the "Father" at the same moment. Likewise, the divine Spirit finds itself involved with the responses of creatures as well as with the response of the "Son" to the "Father." Finally, the "Father" can offer a more nuanced set of initial aims, given the fact of creation and the existence of finite subjects of experience.

All of this interaction between the divine persons and their creatures is possible only because from the beginning they all share a common field of activity, a "place," so to speak, where they can encounter one another and in different ways influence each other's processes of concrescence. Furthermore, each actual occasion by definition retains its own individual identity even as it contributes its "decision" or objectification to the overall structure of the common field of activity. The divine persons, of course, contribute much more to the structure of that field than any individual finite occasion or indeed than all of them together. But the point is that within the framework of a field occasions of various kinds can co-exist and produce a common effect.

Consider by way of contrast the image of the God-world relationship that Whitehead offers in *Process and Reality*. God and finite occasions are pictured as initially opposed to one another in their separate processes of concrescence. Furthermore, when the finite occasion achieves actuality, it is absorbed immediately into God as the sole actual entity that survives the passage of time. In effect, then, Whitehead is still working, albeit unconsciously so, with an Aristotelian mind-set. That is, implicitly he is thinking of God as a transcendent Substance that at every moment incorporates into itself countless finite actual entities as its latest accidental modifications.[32] All of this flows, moreover, from his decision to regard God as an individual entity rather than as a community of persons who constitute an all-embracing field of activity.

Much the same critique can be exercised with respect to Charles Hartshorne's understanding of the God-world relationship. Admittedly, Hartshorne regarded his own approach as a form of panentheism. In his book *The Divine Relativity*, for example, he says that panentheism "is an appropriate term for the view that deity is in some real aspect distinguishable from and independent of any and all relative items, and yet, taken as an actual whole, includes all relative items."[33] His own approach to the God-world relationship is panentheistic because, while God must be related to some world, God is not necessarily related to this world and its contingent events. Panentheism for Hartshorne, in other words, involves God's freedom from any given world; but it says nothing about the ontological independence of creatures in the world from God. Yet this, too, is part of the notion of panentheism. Everything exists in God and through the power of God. Yet the world and all finite entities within it are separate from God, existing in their own right.

Hartshorne presumably does not discuss this other meaning of panentheism because, in line with Whitehead, he holds that in the end only God survives. As soon as finite entities achieve actuality, they are absorbed into God. Hartshorne's concept of God is, to be sure, somewhat different from that of Whitehead. As already noted, he conceives God as a transcendent personally ordered society of occasions rather than as an ever-concrescing transcendent actual entity. As a result, his favorite model for the God-world relationship is that of the soul and the body within human beings. Just as the soul is a society of personally ordered occasions that gives coherence and unity to the various societies of living and nonliving actual occasions within the human body, so God as a transcendent society of actual occasions gives coherence and unity to the myriad number of societies of occasions making up the world.[34] There is, however, a key difference between the body-soul relationship and the God-world relationship, which Hartshorne seems to have overlooked. Whereas in Hartshorne's psychology the human soul likewise perishes with the death of the body, in his understanding of the God-world relationship, God does not perish with the demise of any given world. At least in principle, God simply acquires a new body, a new world with which to be related.

Once again, therefore, we are faced with the unexpected consequences of a line of thought initiated by Whitehead but now carried forward with some modifications by Hartshorne. Like Whitehead, Hartshorne ends up with a picture of God using the world (and all the finite entities in it) as the instrument of God's own life. Within the body-soul relationship as Hartshorne presents it, of course, the soul must look to the needs of the body because its own continued existence depends upon the health of the body. But this is by definition not true of the God-world relationship. God needs some world, but not necessarily this world, to survive. Hence, all of us belonging to this world are reductively only instruments for the ongoing growth and perfection of God. Hartshorne, to be sure, stresses the opposite features of this relationship between God and the world: "Whereas we are left unaffected by the misery or joy of millions we do not know even the existence of, God has nowhere to hide himself from any sorrow or joy whatever, but must share in all the wealth and all the burden of the world."[35] Be that as it may, God alone survives to feel those joys and sorrows in an enduring way. In the end, all creatures are nothing more than accidental modifications of the divine being.

In conclusion, let me state that these critical remarks are not intended to diminish the achievement either of Whitehead or of Hartshorne in working out a consistent process-relational metaphysics. My own hypothesis is clearly dependent upon the results of their sustained reflection upon the God-world relationship. Yet a small mistake in judgment at the beginning can have significant negative consequences in the final analysis. Whitehead's decision to conceive God as an actual *entity* and Hartshorne's decision to conceive God and the world together as a "compound individual"[36] are, in my view, clear examples of such modest mistakes in judgment with notable negative consequences for a deeper understanding of the God-world relationship. The reader, however, will have to make an independent judgment on this matter after she or he has read the final chapter of this book in which I set forth my own theory of the God-world relationship as a cosmic society.

7

The Cosmic Society

There are numerous reasons on religious grounds for believing in subjective immortality for human beings and perhaps for sub-human creation as well. Many people, for example, assert that the heart of the Good News of the Christian Bible is belief in the resurrection of the body; what Jesus experienced on Easter Sunday morning will someday be the common experience of all human beings. Likewise, the theme of life after death is present in the Wisdom literature of the Hebrew Bible and in the Koran, the sacred book of Islam. Furthermore, if one includes all those religions whose rituals make reference to a spirit world or the world of the ancestors, then, one could argue that the desire for unending life is well-nigh universal among the peoples of the earth. Even within Buddhism, where an official agnosticism about the possibility of life after death prevails, popular piety still fosters belief in various intermediate states between the present life and Nirvana, the final absorption of the self into Ultimate Reality.[1]

The argument to be made in this chapter for life after death, however, will be purely philosophical. As already indicated in the foreword, the new cosmology that I have in mind is based on a panentheistic understanding of the God-world relationship. In chapter 6, I made clear how panentheism is vindicated in princi-ple as soon as one accepts a field-oriented approach to reality. For, if the three divine persons of the Christian Trinity co-con-stitute by their interrelated activity an all-inclusive field within which the activities of all finite entities are located, and if the decisions of the divine persons from moment to moment impact upon their creatures and the self-constituting decisions of crea-tures are felt by the divine persons, then, one may legitimately say that God and creatures occupy a common world, a joint field of activity that all of them assist in shaping and forming. Because of the primacy of the reality of God, creatures, to be sure, first come into being through the power of God. But they subse-

quently exist in their own right and make their individual contribution to the field of activity that they share with the divine
persons.

At the same time, if these finite actual occasions perish as soon
as they complete their individual processes of concrescence,
then, the notion of a common world for God and creatures is
severely limited. Through the objectifications that their self-constituting decisions produced in the common field of activity, of
course, finite occasions continue to have an impact both upon
the divine persons in their subsequent decisions and upon future
finite occasions in their concrescence. But these occasions themselves have perished in their subjective immediacy and are thus
no longer members, in the full sense, of the world that they
helped to create. Reductively, then, the worldview of Whitehead
and Hartshorne reasserts itself: in a world marked by "perpetual
perishing," only God as the transcendent actual entity or the
transcendent set of actual occasions survives.

To complete the picture of a panentheistic universe, therefore,
it is important to propose subjective immortality not only for
human beings but also for all other societies of occasions as well.
For, if one believes in the resurrection of the body, as noted above,
then, logically one should also believe in the subjective immortality of all creation. The human body as a highly complex unity
of societies of living and nonliving actual occasions is a microcosm of the entire universe. Thus, if it survives, then all of
creation should in principle be capable of subjective immortality.
Obviously, the actual occasions constituting physical reality will
not survive in their materiality. As I argued in chapter 2 and
elsewhere, materiality seems to be no more than the way that
later occasions prehend earlier occasions within the space-time
continuum. Presumably when occasions are incorporated into
the communitarian life of the three divine persons, they lose
their materiality and are prehended in their subjective immediacy through their objectifications in the common field of activity. In other words, within the communitarian life of the
divine persons, all completed occasions will prehend one another with the same immediacy and "peculiar completeness"
that successive occasions within human temporal consciousness
prehend their predecessors even now in the space-time continuum.[2]

All this, however, is to anticipate what I shall argue below in
more systematic fashion. To begin my formal treatment of the
issue, I will first recall what Whitehead himself says about the

possibility of subjective immortality for at least some finite occasions. Then I will summarize the arguments of certain Whiteheadians, notably Marjorie Suchocki, that these sparse remarks of the master need to be expanded upon and further developed. Thirdly, I will set forth my own emendations of their remarks with special attention to the trinitarian and field-oriented understanding of the God-world relationship, which I already set forth in chapter 6. Then, in the final section of the chapter, I will indicate the pertinence of this understanding of Ultimate Reality as an all-embracing cosmic society likewise for those Whiteheadians of a more "empirical" bent who are attracted by the thought of Bernard Meland and Bernard Loomer.

In part five of *Process and Reality*, while discussing the consequent nature of God, Whitehead says: "In this way God is completed by the individual, fluent satisfactions of finite fact, and the temporal occasions are completed by their everlasting union with their transformed selves, purged into conformation with the eternal order which is the final absolute 'wisdom.' "[3] What is to be understood by the phrase "their transformed selves"? Does this mean that they retain their subjective immediacy in a transformed state within the divine being? A few pages later, Whitehead makes another statement that seems to point in that direction. Speaking of the "creative phases in which the universe accomplishes its actuality," he remarks: "Thirdly, there is the phase of perfected actuality, in which the many are one everlastingly, without the qualification of any loss either of individual identity or of completeness of unity. In everlastingness, immediacy is reconciled with objective immortality."[4] Neither of these comments are probative, of course, but they do reinforce the idea that in this last part of *Process and Reality* Whitehead was trying to express insights and feelings for which his previously worked out categoreal scheme was no longer fully adequate. Yet, even if this be true, should one give more credence to the vision of reality at the end of the book or to the antecedent categoreal scheme?

Those who put their trust in the categoreal scheme point out that, in discussing the "satisfaction" with which a finite entity terminates its process of concrescence, Whitehead states unequivocally, "No actual entity can be conscious of its own satisfaction; for such knowledge would be a component in the process, and would thereby alter the satisfaction."[5] This would seem to eliminate the possibility of a finite entity retaining subjective immediacy within the consequent nature of God. For, on the one hand, it cannot be prehended by God until it has achieved satisfaction, that is, determinate actuality; on the other hand, as soon as it achieves satisfaction, it ceases to be a subject of experience. It becomes a superject, an object of prehension for God and subsequent finite occasions. Hence, even God cannot prehend it as both subject and superject at the same time. Yet, this is precisely what is needed if God is to prehend the entity in its subjective immediacy and incorporate it as such into the divine consequent nature. Hence, in terms of Whitehead's categoreal scheme, finite occasions can only possess objective immortality within the consequent nature of God because God can only prehend them as superjects after subjective immediacy has ended.

David Griffin and Marjorie Suchocki are two Whiteheadians who have tried to remain basically faithful to the categoreal scheme of the master even as they offer arguments for the possibility of subjective immortality within that scheme. Griffin's argument, to be sure, is limited to subjective immortality for human beings in their temporal consciousness. Since the human psyche even in this life enjoys a certain independence of the body in which it is housed, it seems entirely possible that, freed from the body through death, it could relate to God and other finite selves more directly and immediately than it can in the present life:

> Just as the person in the body can have a strong sense of individuality, of himself as distinct from his body, and yet be intimately related to the body, feeling its experiences sympathetically, and even in a strong sense as his own, so one might in a future existence keep a strong sense of individuality and yet overcome some of the feeling of over-againstness and externality in relation to other selves that so characterizes our present existence.[6]

Suchocki, on the other hand, proposes a minor modification of Whitehead's conceptual scheme that would enable literally every actual occasion to enjoy subjective immortality within the consequent nature of God. Whereas Whitehead stipulated that each occasion is first a subject of experience and then a superject for later occasions, Suchocki suggests that intermediate between these two phases of existence is *enjoyment* where the occasion is a determinate actuality and thus capable of prehension by God and yet still a subject of experience enjoying the completion of its process of concrescence. "Indeterminateness is gone, that is so, but it is now replaced by the fullness of that which is fully actual. . . . It is a conclusion to immediacy that is also the inclusion of immediacy, and not a conclusion bereft of that immediacy. Immediacy is becoming *and* satisfaction: the result, together with its becoming."[7]

Suchocki goes on to argue that, because God prehends the entity in the instant when it is both subject and superject, and because God prehends it in its entirety with no "negative" prehensions, God prehends it in its subjective immediacy and preserves it as such within the divine consequent nature. Implicit therein is the further argument that "negative" prehensions, that is, purely formal prehensions of antecedent occasions without positive impact on the concrescence of the prehending occasion,[8] are necessary for finite occasions because they cannot incorporate the antecedent occasion in its entirety into their own processes of concrescence without loss of their own identity. "The inclusion of the other is always a partial inclusion, and, therefore, always an objective inclusion. To one finite occasion another occasion is always objective."[9] Only God as the transcendent actual entity is able to prehend finite occasions in their entirety, that is, in their subjective immediacy, without loss of self-identity within the divine process of concrescence. God thus is the finite occasion in its subjective immediacy even as God continues to be the divine self. Similarly, the finite occasion within the consequent nature of God is both itself and God. That is, it feels God's feelings for itself even as it continues to feel its own satisfaction in what it has de facto become.

On this basis, Suchocki argues for a progressive transformation in the finite occasion's experience of itself. For, in feeling God's feeling for itself, the occasion becomes aware: first, of what it might have become if it had more perfectly conformed its subjective aim to the divine initial aim for it; secondly, of its role in the society (societies) to which it immediately belongs; and, finally, of its role in relation to the entire world process (or, equivalently, of its role in relation to God).[10] This heightened self-awareness is, of course, also a judgment: initially, the judgment of God upon itself, but in the end its own enlightened self-judgment as it sees for the first time in total objectivity what good it accomplished or failed to accomplish. Yet, because it has de facto been accepted by God and incorporated into the divine consequent nature, the entity finds in the end a sense of peace in its belonging to a whole of incomparably greater worth than itself. "The judgment that flows from the occasion's relation to the whole is finally, then, a knowledge of one's participation and belonging within the completed whole: judgment is transformation, redemption and peace."[11]

One must admire the ingenuity with which Suchocki thus adjusts Whitehead's conceptual scheme so as to allow for subjective immortality for finite occasions. Admittedly, most of her remarks quoted above have reference to those occasions that constitute temporal consciousness or the psyche within human beings. But, in principle, all finite occasions can be prehended by God in their subjective immediacy and be suitably transformed through incorporation into the divine consequent nature. Naturally, the inanimate occasions constituting the great mass of physical nature would not need "redemption" in the same sense as occasions constituting the human psyche, which presumably deviated from the divine initial aim for them, at least in some measure. Nor would those same inanimate occasions experience "peace," if by peace is meant a conscious acceptance of one's participation in a whole greater than oneself. For, if these occasions were not conscious during their concrescence in the space-time continuum, they should not be conscious participants in the divine consequent nature. But they should on a feeling-level experience "transformation," a feeling of well-being consistent with belonging to a higher level of existence than before. I will return to this theme shortly when I consider how to modify Suchocki's presentation so as to incorporate it into my own trinitarian and field-oriented understanding of the God-world relationship.

In the meantime, however, I call attention to one other feature of Suchocki's hypothesis that deserves commendation. Charles Hartshorne has in the past cast doubt on the desirability of subjective immortality for human beings on the grounds that it would in the end be very boring and frustrating for the individuals thus guaranteed indefinite existence into the future. "Each of us is a theme with variations. No theme other than that of the divine nature can admit an infinity of variations all significant enough to be worth making a place for in reality. Life is cumulative; but it is just as true that it is self-exhaustive."[12] Accordingly, unless like God one has an infinite capacity for absorbing novelty and change into one's being without loss of self-identity, eternal life would be most undesirable. For, an indefinitely prolonged series of basically uniform experiences would inevitably result in "ever increasing monotony or boredom."[13] Yet the thrust of Suchocki's presentation is that the finite occasion is not simply itself but one with God within the divine consequent nature. It experiences not only its own feelings, its own limited satisfaction, but God's feelings for it as part of God's feelings for the entire world process up to that moment. As noted above, it thus undergoes a progressive transformation as it more and more accepts itself and its own modest role in the world process in the light of God's feelings for it. Finally, insofar as the divine feelings are constantly being deepened and amended in the light of new events within the world process, it would seem that the finite occasion should likewise experience itself within God in ever new ways. Boredom and monotony are thus effectively excluded because the occasion, without ceasing to be itself, is sharing in the ever-expanding life of God.[14]

But, one may ask, can a given finite occasion refuse to be thus transformed? Suchocki's answer is no. As she comments:

It is God's subjectivity into which the occasion is now incorporated, and hence God's subjective aim and God's own freedom governs the process. The occasion is therefore not free to accept or reject its completion within God, for freedom belongs with the concrescing subject. This is now God. The occasion's freedom was exercised in its finite process of becoming, and was exhausted in the process. Hence its incorporation is an incorporation into the freedom of God.[15]

This is certainly consistent with her exposition of the stage of "enjoyment" as intermediate between the subjective process of concrescence and the state of being a superject, that is, an object of prehension for later occasions. The occasion can only enjoy what it has already become; it cannot alter its determinate actuality as fixed by the "decision" ending the process of concrescence.

Yet it also paradoxically seems to provide for a doctrine of hell (or at least a prolonged state of purgatory) within Suchocki's scheme. For, in the sentence immediately following the above quotation, she notes, "Insofar as the occasion's finite decision moved in conformity with God's own desires for it, then the occasion's experience of God's freedom would be experienced as an extension and fulfillment of its own freedom; insofar as its finite decision was contrary to God's purposes, the experience of God's freedom would be felt as the restriction of its own."[16] Feeling one's self-constituting decision called into question by a higher power and being helpless to revise it would count as damnation in the eyes of many. But presumably what Suchocki has in mind here is that the occasion could over a period of time

revise its feelings about its decision even if it could not revise the
decision itself. Hence, it could over a period of time come peace-
fully to accept its somewhat (or even largely) negative role in the
overall world process and thus find "enjoyment" in God and the
fulfillment of the world process despite itself.[17] In any event,
from these and other passages it is clear that the experience of a
finite occasion within the consequent nature of God would not in
any sense of the word be monotonous or boring.

At this point, I turn to an exposition of my own understanding
of how finite occasions constitute with the divine persons an
ever-expanding cosmic society that is, in effect, Ultimate Reality
within my scheme. I begin by stating that I accept Suchocki's
revision of Whitehead's categoreal scheme, as summarized above.
That is, with Suchocki I believe that God does prehend finite
occasions not simply as superjects or inanimate objects of prehension, but as subjects of experience enjoying the completion of
their individual process of concrescence. Likewise, I accept the
hypothesis that finite occasions thus taken up into the divine life
undergo a process of transformation or conversion whereby they
gradually come to accept what they have become, that is, their
self-constituting decisions in the space-time continuum, as a
tiny part of a much greater whole that continues to expand with
the addition of new generations of actual occasions. If one would
object that such a conversion process would involve new prehensions and therefore a new process of concrescence for the occasions in question, my response would be, as noted above, that the
self-constituting decisions of the occasions are not thereby altered; only the degree of self-acceptance is altered as the occasions progressively learn to make God's feelings in their regard
the basis for their own feelings about themselves. Admittedly,
there remains some ambiguity here if one adheres strictly to the
categoreal scheme of Whitehead. But, as already noted, in part
five of *Process and Reality* Whitehead seems to be saying the
same thing as I am here: "God is completed by the individual,
fluent satisfactions of finite fact, and the temporal occasions are
completed by their everlasting union with their transformed
selves, purged into conformation with the eternal order which is
the final absolute 'wisdom.'"[18]

In any event, my principal task in this part of the chapter will
be to show how Suchocki's reinterpretation of Whitehead in favor
of subjective immortality for finite occasions makes even more
sense within the trinitarian and field-oriented approach to the
God-world relationship that I set forth earlier. First of all, it

seems clear to me that Suchocki's scheme would benefit from an understanding of God as a community of three divine persons. For, in that case, as I pointed out in chapter 6, the community of redeemed finite occasions can be incorporated into the already existing community of the divine persons so as to constitute an all-embracing cosmic society. The divine community is thus both the ontological foundation and the model for all human communities. Elsewhere in her book, to be sure, Suchocki says that God is a community, meaning the community of all transformed finite occasions.[19] But this only illustrates the ambiguity of maintaining that one and the same reality is both a transcendent individual entity and a community of finite individuals. Reductively, the one concept must be subordinate to the other.

In the first case, if God is fundamentally conceived as an individual entity, then the finite entities gathered into community within the divine consequent nature are logically accidental modifications of God's own being as an individual existent. For, as I noted above in chapter 6, choosing to regard God as an individual entity (Whitehead) or God and the world together as a "compound individual" (Harthshorne) is implicitly to be thinking in a classical mind-set in which there exist only individual things or substances. If one substance is somehow incorporated into another substance, then the first substance (for example, a human being or other finite entity) loses its substantial form and becomes part of the reality of the other substance (the divine being). In the second case, on the other hand, if God is conceived primarily as a community of finite entities and only secondarily, if at all, as an individual entity, then "God" seems to be no more than the religiously derived name for the community of finite entities. This is the pancosmism to which I made reference in the foreword and to which I will return later in this chapter when discussing the cosmologies of Bernard Meland and Bernard Loomer. For the moment, I simply wish to emphasize that the only way to avoid the Scylla of pantheism and the Charybdis of pancosmism in working out a genuinely panentheistic understanding of the God-world relationship is to envision God as a community of divine persons within whose all-comprehensive field of activity the field proper to the community of all finite entities has its place.

More specifically, however, how does the field-oriented approach to Whiteheadian societies advanced in this book allow one to say that Ultimate Reality is a cosmic society, a society of subsocieties, each of which makes its contribution to the unity of the whole? Fields by definition include subfields and normally are themselves contained within even larger fields. As Whitehead comments in *Process and Reality*:

> There is no society in isolation. Every society must be considered with its background of a wider environment of actual entities, which also contribute their objectifications to which the members of the society must conform. Thus the given contributions of the environment must at least be permissive of the self-sustenance of the society. Also, in proportion to its importance, this background must contribute those general characters which the more special character of the society presupposes for its members.[20]

What Whitehead has in mind here is the way in which the laws governing the larger field of activity influence the behavior of entities within smaller, more specialized fields of activity. But the converse must likewise be true, namely, that the self-constituting decisions of entities within the smaller fields of activity likewise impact upon the laws governing the larger fields of activity and the entities constitutive of those fields. The inanimate actual occasions within the human body, for example, through their self-constituting decisions impact upon the operation of the soul as the presiding set of occasions within the body, even as the soul through the decisions of its constituent occasions influences the self-constitution of successive generations of inanimate occasions within the body.

In terms of the God-world relationship, what this implies is that the three divine persons and all their creatures possess an ontological independence of one another and yet co-constitute a common world. The world or field of activity proper to creation is, of course, smaller and more constrained than the field proper to the three divine persons, which is co-terminous with the extensive continuum. But, insofar as the decisions of all finite occasions are felt by the three divine persons in their relations to one another and the decisions of the divine persons influence the decisions of all finite occasions in their world, then, at least in part, the divine persons and their creatures occupy a common world. The three divine persons, in other words, do not in themselves constitute Ultimate Reality; rather, the divine persons plus all their creatures constitute Ultimate Reality. The society of the divine persons is only a subsociety, albeit the most important subsociety, within Ultimate Reality, understood as an all-embracing cosmic society. For, all societies of finite occasions likewise contribute to the ongoing existence and structure of this cosmic society. In that sense, the divine persons and all their creatures are co-creators of a common world. As I see it, this is the ideal aimed at in the notion of panentheism.

Furthermore, the field-oriented approach to the God-world relationship set forth in this book helps to explain how finite occasions within the divine consequent nature can grasp their predecessor occasions not serially, as in the space-time continuum, but simultaneously. For Suchocki, this was accomplished for the finite occasion by God, in that upon entrance into the divine consequent nature, the entity felt God's feelings not only for itself but for all its predecessors at the same time. But this seems to beg the question of how God grasps in simultaneity what came into existence serially. The notion of a society as a preexisting field for the emergence of new occasions, however, solves this problem quite nicely both for the divine persons and for all personally ordered finite occasions. The new actual occasion grasps its predecessors in and through their objectifications in the field. In prehending the field as structured one way rather than another, the occasion grasps both the objectifications and the subjective immediacies that they represent.

At one point in her exposition, Suchocki seems indirectly to say the same thing: "The way an entity prehends the past—objectively or subjectively—depends primarily upon the needs of the prehending entity and the consequent ability or inability of the entity to prehend other occasions in their entirety."[21] Within the space-time continuum, where the needs of the finite occasion are to prehend predecessor occasions in their larger configurations or "materiality," prehension of the subjective immediacy of those same occasions would be a source of confusion and ambiguity. Within the divine consequent nature, however, especially if this be understood as an all-embracing field of activity where materiality is no longer a factor, then the finite occasion (like the three divine persons) can prehend the field as a structured whole, in effect, read the past history of the society to which it belongs in the structure of the field, and thereby identify with all the previous subjectivities therein represented. Furthermore, like the three divine persons, it does not have to identify with each previous subjectivity serially in order to feel the impact of that subjectivity upon its own actuality here and now.

As I mentioned earlier in the chapter, the closest analogy that we humans living in the space-time continuum have with this special type of intersubjective experience is the way in which we identify with our own past selves within temporal consciousness. Despite all the intervening weeks, months, even years, we feel that we are basically the same person that we were at that previous moment. We feel, in other words, the impact of that other subjectivity upon our present subjectivity much more immediately and directly than we feel the impact of other human beings, even those immediately present to us here and now. Thus even within the space-time continuum, we experience some freedom from the limits of prehension according to the mode of pure objectivity or materiality. In the experience of our own selfhood, past and present, seriality is, at least to a certain extent, superseded by simultaneity even now.

Still another argument in favor of the field-oriented approach to the God-world relationship runs as follows. As noted above, every human being or indeed any physical organism is a subfield within a complex hierarchy of structured fields of activity: for example, the field proper to some local community or environment, to our planet, to creation as a whole, and, finally, to the all-embracing activity of the three divine persons. But as a specialized subfield of activity, the human being is an objective reality within the more comprehensive objective realities of the local community, the earth, creation as a whole and the world of the three divine persons. Whereas Suchocki proposes that the unity of the created world and of all the societal realities within that world is grounded in the unity of the divine Selfhood, I am thus suggesting that the unity of the all-embracing cosmic society is the dynamic unity of all the interrelated subsocieties. There is, accordingly, a basic difference in the relationship between the One and the Many in the two schemes.

Suchocki's (and Whitehead's) scheme for the unity of the God-world relationship is more in line with classical metaphysics which, following Plato, proposes that the unity of the empirical Many is grounded in a common relationship to a transcendent One. For Plato, the realities of common sense experience are grounded in their intelligible Forms, which are themselves grounded in the Idea of the Good.[22] This same idea was basically carried forward in Aristotle's proposal that the immaterial substantial form is the principle of unity for the material elements. Likewise, it became the basis for the understanding of the God-world relationship at the hands of Thomas Aquinas and other Christian metaphysicians. Eventually, this mind-set was challenged by Martin Heidegger who, as already noted in the introduction, reviewed the history of Western metaphysics and declared that ontology was in effect onto-theology; the study of Being had become the study of the Supreme Being. Subsequent to Heidegger, many contemporary philosophers and even some theologians have eliminated any references to God as a transcendent being in their thinking and concentrated exclusively on the world process as a subsistent reality in its own right.

My own proposal for the unity of the God-world relationship is partly grounded in the judgment that Heidegger and other contemporary thinkers are correct in rejecting this older paradigm for the relationship of the One and the Many. But it is also grounded in my reading of the Whiteheadian concept of society as elaborated in this book whereby the One is emergent out of the interrelated activities of the Many vis-à-vis one another. Ironically, however, neither Whitehead himself nor most Whiteheadians seemed to have grasped the full implications of this doctrine of society. For, Whitehead (and Suchocki), as noted above, grounded the God-world relationship in the older understanding of the relationship between the One and the Many; the unity of the many finite occasions is grounded in their common relationship to God as the divine Self. Hartshorne, to be sure, modified Whitehead's understanding of the God-world relationship so as to make it conformable with the classical understanding of the relationship between the soul and body. But this is still based on the older paradigm of the transcendent One communicating its unity of existence and activity to the empirical Many. Only the pancosmists among the Whiteheadians (for example, Meland and Loomer) have definitively moved to the newer paradigm for the relationship between the One and the Many. But, in so doing, they seem to have implicitly, if not explicitly, surrendered belief in a personal God. My own conviction, of course, is that one can still retain belief in a personal God within this new paradigm for the One and the Many, provided that one thinks of God in trinitarian terms as a community of divine persons who share a common field of activity with their creatures. Keeping this in mind, I turn now to a brief consideration of the thought of Meland and Loomer.

In *Fallible Forms and Symbols*, Meland offers the following reflections on his own understanding of God:

> The nexus of relationships that forms our existence is not projected, it is given. We do not create these relationships; we experience them, being given with existence. And from this Matrix come resources of

grace that can carry us beyond the meanings of our own making, and alert us to goodness that is not of our own willing or defining. This goodness in existence which we do not create, but which creates and saves us, is the datum to which I attend. It is literally a work of judgment and grace, a primordial and provident goodness, the efficacy of which may be discerned in every event of creativity, sensitivity, and negotiability. Thus I am led empirically to speak of God as the Ultimate Efficacy within relationships.[23]

What Meland is describing, of course, is the strictly empirical meaning of God, the way that God is normally experienced by human beings in daily life. He deliberately avoids any metaphysical or ontological understanding of God that cannot be verified in ordinary experience. As such, God is both one and many. As Ultimate Efficacy or Creative Passage, God is the transcendent principle for the entire world process. But God concretely exists only in the empirical Many, that is, in the de facto relationships of finite entities to one another from moment to moment.[24] Thus for Meland God is equivalent to what Whitehead called Creativity. But this means that Creativity no longer is the intermediary between God and the World, as with Whitehead.[25] Rather, only the World exists and God (Creativity) is its transcendent principle of becoming.

I am not suggesting here that Meland is an atheist; his description of Ultimate Efficacy as "a work of judgment and grace, a primordial and provident goodness" testifies to his belief in God. But the logic of his strictly empirical approach to the God-world relationship leads him effectively to identify God with the world process, just as the logic of the more a priori or postulational approach of Whitehead, Harshorne and Suchocki led them ultimately to collapse the world into God. Would my own field-oriented approach to the God-world relationship be helpful here to maintain an empirical approach to the God-world relationship such as Meland espouses and yet to avoid pancosmism, the ultimate identification of God with the world? I believe that it would for the following reasons.

First of all, within a field-oriented approach to reality, each of the subfields is governed by its own laws and possesses its own relative autonomy even as it contributes to the larger field of activity that constitutes the greater whole. Applied to the God-world relationship, this means that the world of creation is a functioning totality within the field of activity proper to the divine persons. A strictly empirical or experiential approach to reality should therefore directly encompass the totality proper to creation with its laws and modes of operation. But, only indirectly, if indeed at all, should that empirical approach to reality be aware of the broader field of activity proper to the divine persons. For, the presence and activity of the divine persons has to be mediated by the laws and structural principles of the world of creation, if that subordinate totality is to maintain its relative autonomy and independent mode of operation. Hence, when Meland, Loomer, and other empirically oriented Whiteheadians claim that they have no experience of God as an entity separate from the world, they are exactly correct. God is not an entity within the world of creation that can be directly felt or experienced. Rather, if God is experienced at all, God is felt as an influence upon the world of creation, so to speak, from the outside. Yet, even that influence has to be exerted in and through the laws and operational principles proper to the sphere of creation. Thus, for one not inclined or otherwise prepared to feel this mediated influence of God upon the world, experience yields only knowledge of the world.

Meland, however, claims for Ultimate Efficacy more than what Whitehead claims for Creativity. As noted above, he experiences Ultimate Efficacy as "a work of judgment and grace, a primordial and provident goodness," whereas for Whitehead Creativity is an impersonal principle of Becoming that is operative to produce evil as well as good within the world process.[26] This would seem to be an instance of the mediated experience of God, as mentioned above. For, in itself a principle of Becoming, as Whitehead claims, is a purely functional reality, unable to distinguish between good and evil in the effects that it brings about. Hence, if it is experienced as beneficent rather than neutral in its mode of operation, then something (someone) else is simultaneously being experienced as well. From the perspective of my own trinitarian understanding of the God-world relationship, I would say that Meland is experiencing the activity of the Holy Spirit upon the world as mediated through the principle of Creativity operative in the world of creation. As I already indicated in chapter 6, the Holy Spirit is linked in a special way with the principle of Creativity within the divine sphere of activity. Hence, it seems appropriate that the Spirit should be active in the world of creation through that same principle, personalizing it so that it will be experienced by Meland and others as "a primordial and provident goodness."

In any event, the field-oriented approach to the God-world

relationship provides a theoretical justification for Meland's claims as to the nature of Ultimate Efficacy. "This goodness in existence which we do not create, but which creates and saves us" bears mute testimony to a larger field of activity than that proper to creation. Moreover, this larger field with its own laws and structural principles (based, as I see it, on the interrelated activity of the three divine persons vis-à-vis one another) has an indirect but still very significant influence upon the self-constitution of finite entities within the field proper to creation.

I turn now to an analysis of Bernard Loomer's understanding of the God-world relationship, above all, as set forth in his controversial essay, "The Size of God." Like Meland, Loomer employs a strictly empirical approach to the notion of the God-world relationship. Accordingly, like Meland, he comes to the conclusion that God is not experienced as separate from the world. Rather, God is to be identified with the totality of the world process. Most interesting for our purposes in this book, however, he then further specifies the world as "a generalized enduring society," a vast network of subsocieties.[27] Loomer, in other words, is describing the world much as I have presented it in this chapter, namely, as a cosmic society, but without reference to the three divine persons who constitute the principal subsociety within this cosmic totality. This is to be expected, of course, since the activity of the three divine persons in our regard is mediated through the events and relationships constitutive of our world from moment to moment.

Yet, as John Cobb indicates in his commentary on Loomer's essay, Loomer calls the world "God" because implicitly he has more than the world as a concrete actuality in mind.[28] Loomer himself says:

> The world is God because it is the source and preserver of meaning; because the creative advance of the world in its adventure is the supreme cause to be served; because even in our desecration of our space and time within it, the world is holy ground; and because it contains and yet enshrouds the ultimate mystery inherent within existence itself.[29]

Clearly, something more than the world as a concrete actuality is being mediated to Loomer through such an experience of the world. From the perspective of my own theory, I would suggest that Loomer is implicitly experiencing the trinitarian structure of the world: its origin at every moment in the initial aims of the

"Father," its de facto unity with the "Son" in the "Son's" ongoing response to the "Father," and its experience of self-transcendence in and through the mediating activity of the Holy Spirit. But, apart from this specifically trinitarian hypothesis, one may safely say that a field-oriented approach to the God-world relationship would allow Loomer thus to affirm that the world is both itself and more than itself at the same time. The field proper to creation is nested within an even broader field of activity which, however, can only be experienced by human beings indirectly in terms of mystical feelings and desires.

Loomer himself gives expression to such mystical feelings when, at the very end of his essay, he describes the world as "an interconnected web endeavouring to become a vast socialized unit of experience with its own processive subjectivity."[30] The world as such does not "endeavour" to become anything since it lacks a subjectivity proper to itself. Hence, if Loomer experiences a transpersonal subjectivity at work in the world, it can only be the subjectivity of God or, in my scheme, the three divine persons progressively incorporating the world of creation into their own communitarian life.[31]

One other feature of Loomer's presentation of God as the world should be considered before bringing this analysis of his thought in "The Size of God" to a close. Because God is identical with the world and because the world itself is riddled with ambiguity in terms of the long-term meaning and value of the events that take place within it, then, says Loomer, the reality of God is likewise ambiguous. God is not unequivocally to be identified with what from a human standpoint is rational and good. God shares the ambiguity of the world; but, for that very same reason, God grows in stature or size. "An ambiguous God is of greater stature than an unambiguous deity."[32] While agreeing with Loomer that the events that take place in the world are very often ambiguous in terms of their long-range meaning and value, I do not fully concur in his further conclusion that the reality of God is thereby also rendered ambiguous. Insofar as the reality of God is bound up with the reality of the world, it is indeed ambiguous; but, insofar as it is not circumscribed by the reality of the world, it remains unambiguously good and perfect. By way of explanation for this statement, I refer once again to my field-oriented understanding of the God-world relationship.

The world of creation is a semiautonomous field of activity within the all-embracing field of activity proper to the three divine persons. Within their own field of activity, that is, in terms of their ongoing interpersonal relationships to one another, the three divine persons experience no ambiguity whatsoever. By definition, they have an unlimited knowledge of one another's subjectivities and complete good will in maintaining their life together as a divine community. Accordingly, all the reasons for ambiguity that are grounded in the finitude of human knowledge or in the instability of human decision-making are lacking when one considers the perfection of the divine community. Nor is there good reason to suspect their motives in dealing with us, their creatures. The presumption should be that the divine intention in our regard is always honorable and good, if only because the divine persons have nothing to gain from deceitful and underhanded behavior in our regard. In creating our world, they acted out of self-giving love, not personal need. Hence, given the unlimited character of their knowledge and love for us, their creatures, there is no good reason to suspect their intentions in our regard.

The concrete results of their activity in our regard, however, are frequently ambiguous because the three divine persons cannot unilaterally execute their decisions in our regard. That is, they share with us humans and indeed with all their creatures a common world, the world of creation that is co-constituted at every moment by all the actual occasions (finite and infinite) in existence at that instant. The results of such an enormous confluence of self-constituting decisions must invariably be ambiguous. Much good is indeed accomplished; the world of creation is sustained in existence as part of the divine "Son's" ongoing response to the "Father" in the power of the Spirit. But much evil likewise comes into being at the same time, which will inevitably have a negative impact upon the concrescence of subsequent generations of actual occasions within the world process.

For, as noted above, even after incorporation into the divine communitarian life, these same occasions can for a time resist divine acceptance and thus thwart their complete integration into the unity of the cosmic society. They cannot, to be sure, alter the objective reality of the society that they have helped to constitute. But, through their negative feelings toward the role that they themselves played in its formation, they can pass on to subsequent occasions still in process of concrescence within the space-time continuum a type of causal efficacy that is negative as well as positive. What I am presuming here is that past occasions are "given" for prehension by their successors in God, if by "God" is meant the cosmic society in which occasions retain their subjective immediacy and yet, as noted above, are gradually transformed in their feelings about themselves through progressive conformity to the divine feelings in their regard.[33] Insofar as this conformation to the divine feelings about themselves is not complete, these past occasions will be experienced by present occasions in partially negative terms, that is, in an ambiguous manner. After all, what the present occasions are experiencing simultaneously is the harmony of the divine being and the relative disharmony of a world of completed finite occasions still in process of transformation.

Nor is there reason to think that this ambiguity will quickly be dispelled by the passage of time. For, as earlier occasions become more attuned to the divine wisdom in their regard, later occasions will still be struggling to accept their incorporation into the divine communitarian life with equanimity, if not total peace. In this respect, Loomer is at least partially correct in claiming for ambiguity the status of a metaphysical principle.[34] It is an inevitable feature of a world created by the interplay of finite self-constituting subjects of experience. But the ambiguity does not extend to that part of the cosmic society that is occupied by the three divine persons in their relations to one another. As noted above, "Father," "Son," and Holy Spirit experience no ambiguity whatsoever in their life together. Furthermore, as finite occasions become more and more incorporated into the divine communitarian life, they, too, no longer experience ambiguity in their feelings about themselves and the world to which they belong. As Suchocki comments, "the essence of an occasion's union with God is its final bursting of the bonds of selfhood even while affirming that selfhood: the language is not paradoxical, for the reference is simply to a self, a value, which *is* in its givingness, its relatedness to a whole which by far transcends it."[35]

Thus ambiguity is not the last word about the nature of reality, as Loomer's essay might lead one to believe. It is simply the de facto characteristic of the world of space and time and of that part of the cosmic society still undergoing incorporation into the divine communitarian life. Loomer's purely empirical approach to reality does not allow him directly to experience higher levels of existence and activity where ambiguity is no longer operative. Whitehead, however, in his description of "Peace" at the end of *Adventures of Ideas* seems, in fact, to have achieved that higher level of experience:

> The Peace that is here meant is not the negative conception of anaesthesia. It is a positive feeling which crowns the "life and motion"

of the soul. . . . It is not a hope for the future, nor is it an interest in
present details. It is a broadening of feeling due to the emergence of
some deep metaphysical insight, unverbalized and yet momentous in
its coordination of values. . . . Thus Peace carries with it a surpassing
of personality. There is an inversion of relative values. It is primarily a
trust in the efficacy of Beauty.[36]

With these remarks about what I have called the "pancosmism" of Meland and Loomer, I believe that my task both in
this chapter and in the third part of the book is completed. I
began chapter 6 by stating that I would use the notions of *society*
and *spirit* as developed in parts one and two in order to set forth
an understanding of the God-world relationship that would correspond to what is meant by *panentheism*: God immanent in the
world and the world immanent in God without loss to the independent status of either God or the world. My governing hypothesis was that a genuinely panentheistic understanding of the
God-world relationship will only be achieved if one thinks of
God and the world as interpenetrating fields of activity with the
field proper to creation contained within the even larger field of
the divine intentional activity.

To substantiate that hypothesis, I first summarized my understanding of the God-world relationship as set forth in my earlier
book, *The Triune Symbol*. Therein I presented the reality of God
in Whiteheadian terms as a structured society of three personally
ordered subsocieties corresponding to the three divine persons
of Christian tradition. Their unity as one God was thus the
objective unity of a Whiteheadian structured society that I pictured as three circles touching one another in the overall shape of
an equilateral triangle. Within the circle proper to the divine
"Son" I located two other concentric circles, the one within the
other, corresponding to the reality of creation and the human
race respectively. Such a process-oriented and communitarian
understanding of the God-world relationship I was then easily
able to transpose into a field-oriented approach to reality using
the insights acquired in parts one and two of the present manuscript. Finally, in the concluding pages of the chapter, I tried to
show how this field-oriented approach to the God-world relationship is superior to the models for that same relationship
chosen by Whitehead and Hartshorne. For, both of them in different ways conceive God as an individual existent that continually absorbs the contents of the world into itself and thus
alone survives the passage of time. My conclusion was that,
while Whitehead and Hartshorne are not pantheists in the strict

sense, they are likewise not panentheists since the reality of the world within their philosophies is transient and ephemeral by comparison with the reality of God.

Then in chapter 7 I continued this argument for a field-oriented understanding of the God-world relationship by explaining how finite actual occasions upon completion of their process of concrescence in the space-time continuum are prehended in their subjective immediacy by the three divine persons and thus incorporated into the divine communitarian life. Together, the three divine persons and all their creatures from time immemorial thus make up an ever-expanding cosmic society that constitutes Ultimate Reality in my scheme. My chief ally in this task was Suchocki who in her recent book, *The End of Evil*, had already set forth an argument for the subjective immortality of finite occasions within the divine consequent nature. The aim in this part of the chapter was, accordingly, to transpose her scheme into my own and to show how her own hypothesis makes better sense within a field-oriented understanding of the God-world relationship.

Finally, in the last part of the present chapter, I attended to the cosmological theories of Meland and Loomer who, as I saw it, succumbed to still another of the dangers inherent in working out a doctrine of panentheism. That is, whereas Whitehead, Hartshorne and Suchocki had radically subordinated the reality of the world to the enduring reality of God, Meland and Loomer collapsed the reality of God into the reality of the world as an ongoing process. Once again, however, using the field-oriented approach to the God-world relationship, I was able to show how one can indeed affirm the reality of the world as a cosmic society and yet retain belief in God as three divine persons within whose field of intentional activity the world as a complex structured society is located. In this way, the field-oriented approach to the God-world relationship seems to bridge the gap between two disparate schools of process-oriented thought that owe a common debt to Whitehead but have developed in clearly contrary directions in recent years.

All that remains is to offer some thoughts on the pertinence of this field-oriented approach to reality for a broader audience than professionals in the area of process philosophy and theology. To make clear, however, the tentative and still incomplete character of these remarks, I will present them by way of an appendix to the present chapter.

Appendix

The Cosmic Society and the Divine Pleroma

For many English-speaking Roman Catholics, the publication of *The Phenomenon of Man* by the French Jesuit, Pierre Teilhard de Chardin, shortly after his death in 1955 was an event of great symbolic significance. For in their eyes it represented a victory for creative thinking over the innate conservativism of an entrenched ecclesiastical bureaucracy. Be that as it may, the immense popularity that this book subsequently enjoyed added notably to the reputation of Teilhard in the field of cosmology. Indeed, many professional philosophers and scientists who were critical of various details in Teilhard's cosmological scheme nevertheless warmly applauded his efforts to achieve a synthesis "of the material and physical world with the world of mind and spirit; of the past with the future; and of variety with unity, the many with the one."[1] In the intervening years, popular appreciation for the vision of Teilhard still runs strong, especially among liberally oriented Roman Catholics. But critical voices, especially among professional philosophers and scientists, have also been heard with increasing frequency. Stephen Toulmin, for example, to whom reference was made in the preface, is quite skeptical of the validity of Teilhard's key notion of "orthogenesis," that is, an implicit directionality to the world process so as to produce, first life, then rational life, and finally interpersonal life in union with the cosmic Christ. As Toulmin sees it, Teilhard's stipulation of a Christocentric "Omega-Point" is neither good science nor good theology.[2]

Here I believe that the hypothesis of the present book may be of some help to students of Teilhard in responding to critics like Toulmin. For, on the one hand, the notion of a constantly expanding cosmic society of finite existents who enjoy subjective immortality with the three divine persons of the Christian Trinity seems sufficiently close to what Teilhard had in mind with the Divine Pleroma, the recapitulation of all things in Christ. On the other hand, the categoreal scheme of Whitehead, while not being any more "scientific" in the strict sense than Teilhard's, is nevertheless worked out with considerably more rigour and comprehensiveness. Likewise, at least *prima facie*, it is less anthropocentric than Teilhard's scheme, appealing more to general features of Nature than to the unique development of a single species within Nature. Finally, it is less explicitly teleological in its vision of the cosmic process; that is, it does not pretend to predict how the world will come to an end. All of these features of Whitehead's scheme, as I see it, have a certain appeal to rational objectivity and thus would be helpful to Teilhardians as they try to justify the cosmological insights of the master to the general public. Likewise, critics of Teilhard like Toulmin might have to reconsider their prior judgment that his thought represents neither good science nor good theology, if some way were found to express his vision within the more demanding conceptual scheme of Whitehead.

Admittedly, there are problems connected with the attempt to blend the thought of two highly creative individuals. Teilhard, for example, was clearly more of an Aristotelian than Whitehead. That is, he believed that the world process as a whole like every entity within it possesses an entelechy, that is, an immanent purpose or directionality that directs its advance into the future. But he also specified that this goal, Omega Point, is even now being achieved in human history.[3] Hence, Teilhard implicitly endorsed the process-oriented understanding of reality so characteristic of Whitehead even as (in line with Aristotle) he directed his attention more to the future of that process than to its present actuality.

Likewise, Whitehead, without being nearly so anthropocentric in his thinking as Teilhard, nevertheless spoke of a "general purpose pervading nature," namely, the growth of complex structured societies in which intensity of satisfaction for the constituent occasions is combined with greater chance of survival for the society as a whole into the future.[4] Thus the hypothesis of a gradual evolution of the human race toward ever more complex forms of community life is certainly not foreign to Whitehead's cosmological scheme, even though not demanded by it as with Teilhard. Similarly, if one accepts my own reinterpretation of Whiteheadian categories so as to allow, first, for a trinitarian understanding of God as a community of divine persons and, then, for subjective immortality for all finite occasions within that divine communitarian life, one could possibly incorporate much of Teilhard's cosmological vision within the Whiteheadian categoreal scheme to the enrichment of both systems of thought.

This appears even more likely when one considers the striking similarity in the basic metaphysical categories of the two men. For Whitehead, the basic categories are the many, the one, and creativity; for Teilhard, they are plurality, unity, and energy.[5] Both, accordingly, are convinced of the "profoundly 'atomic' character of the universe."[6] But each likewise sees the world as an interconnected whole, a system of quasi-infinite interrelated parts in ordered stages of development, through the all-pervasive activity of what Whitehead calls creativity and Teilhard terms energy. Yet, as noted above, these are only tentative observations. Much more careful work must be done in order to see whether a synthesis such as I have sketched here is indeed realistically possible or even desirable. For, in the end, what is important is not the synthesis of existing systems, but rather the continued growth and further development of process-relational metaphysics as a new and very promising way to understand the world in which we live.

The Cosmic Society and Absolute Emptiness

In recent years, there has been a notable increase in interreligious dialogue between Christian theologians and representatives of various Eastern religions. As James Fredericks comments, members of the Kyoto School of Buddhist philosophy have been especially prominent in this dialogue.[7] Many of them have studied in Europe or the United States and learned quite well the history of Western philosophy and theology. Thus they are in a singularly favorable position to present the insights of their own Buddhist tradition to Westerners in Western categories.

One of these Japanese philosophers is Keiji Nishitani, who studied in Freiburg, West Germany, under the direction of Martin Heidegger from 1936 to 1939. In his major work, *Religion and Nothingness*, he describes Absolute Emptiness, the Void or, in Japanese, śūnyatā, as follows:

> The field of śūnyatā is the field of a force by virtue of which all things as they are in themselves gather themselves together into one: the field of the possibility of the world. At the same time (and in an elemental sense this comes to the same thing), it is the field of the force by virtue of which a given thing gathers itself together: the field of the possibility of the existence of things.[8]

The Void, therefore, is not itself a being but the reality in virtue of which all entities come into existence and are mutually interrelated. It is a field in that it is the necessary context or environment for the emergence and interrelated activity of beings. But it is likewise a force *(virtus)* whereby each of these beings is what it is. As such it is identified with that being's inner self in its "suchness."[9]

In chapter 6 I proposed that the underlying nature of the triune God, the ontological ground for the existence of the three divine persons and all their creatures from moment to moment, is the extensive continuum plus the principle of Creativity. As such, it too could be described as a "force-field" or "the field of the possibility of the existence of things." For, the divine persons and all concrescing finite occasions emerge out of the extensive continuum at every moment through the power of the principle of Creativity. Is it possible, then, that what Nishitani and other Buddhists describe as Absolute Emptiness or the Void is really the underlying nature of the triune God, that which makes possible the slow growth of the cosmic society of all existents, both finite and infinite? If so, then Absolute Emptiness and the cosmic society would be dialectically related to one another as two complementary dimensions of one and the same Ultimate Reality. The cosmic society needs Absolute Emptiness as its ontological ground; Absolute Emptiness requires the cosmic society as its ontological counterpart so as to be an *absolute* emptiness, that is, an emptiness that is simultaneously a fullness.[10]

Once again, however, I must point to the strictly provisional character of these remarks. Much more work will have to be done to verify whether or not Absolute Emptiness can thus be interpreted as the underlying nature of the triune God. Most Buddhists, for example, think of Absolute Emptiness in purely experiential terms, that is, as a profound awareness of the emptiness or nonsubstantiality of the self and all its mental constructions. From that perspective, they would presumably be quite skeptical that one can thus conceive or objectify what in their minds is beyond human comprehension. But Nishitani himself compares Absolute Emptiness with *Gottheit* or the essence of God as described in the writings of the medieval mystic, Meister Eckhart.[11] Hence, there is reason for cautious optimism in continuing to work along these lines. Furthermore, if even moderately successful, this line of thought should prove to be very valuable for the contemporary interreligious dialogue.

Notes

Preface

1. Stephen Toulmin, *The Return to Cosmology: Postmodern Science and the Theology of Nature* (Berkeley: University of California Press, 1985), 1.
2. Ibid., 171.
3. Alfred North Whitehead, *Process and Reality: An Essay in Cosmology*, corrected ed., ed. David Ray Griffin and Donald W. Sherburne (New York: The Free Press, 1978). This text, rather than the original published by Macmillan in 1927, will be used in the present work for page references.
4. Wolfhart Pannenberg, "Atom, Duration, Form: Difficulties with Process Philosophy," *Process Studies* 14 (1984–85): 21.
5. Cf. here George R. Lucas, Jr., "Evolutionist Theories and Whitehead's Philosophy," *Process Studies* 14 (1984–85): 287–300. Lucas conjectures that Whitehead was really not interested in evolution on a cosmological scale, hence, that his relatively sparse references to evolutionary thinkers of the nineteenth and twentieth centuries were not an oversight, but a deliberate choice. Whitehead, in other words, did not want his philosophy of organism to be confused with the highly speculative schemes of the German Idealists and other philosophical cosmologists. Even if this were true, one could still question whether Whitehead made the right choice, i.e., whether one can construct a viable philosophical cosmology without at least some attention to the directionality and goals of the process as a whole. For that matter, in part five of *Process and Reality*, Whitehead seems to address those very questions.
6. Cf. *New Encyclopedia of Philosophy*, ed. J. Grooten and G. Jo Steenbergen, trans. E. van den Bossche (New York: Philosophical Library, 1972), 308–9.
7. Nancy Frankenberry, *Religion and Radical Empiricism* (Albany: State University of New York Press, 1987), esp. 129–56.
8. Whitehead, *Process and Reality*, 340 (517). N.B.: The number in parentheses refers to the pagination in the 1927 edition of *Process and Reality*.

Introduction: Being—Object of Thought or Subject of Experience?

1. Cf., e.g., Richard Rorty, *Philosophy and the Mirror of Nature* (Princeton: Princeton University Press, 1979), 3–13; Jacques Derrida, "Différance," *Margins of Philosophy*, trans. Alan Bass (Chicago: University of Chicago Press, 1982), esp. 21–27.
2. Cf., e.g., Martin Heidegger, "Die Zeit des Weltbildes," *Holzwege*, 6th ed. (Frankfurt am M.: Vittorio Klostermann, 1980), esp. 104–9 (5th *Zusatz*); like-

wise, "Overcoming Metaphysics," *The End of Philosophy*, trans. Joan Stambaugh (New York: Harper & Row, 1973), 87–88.

3. Paul Ricoeur, "The Question of the Subject: The Challenge of Semiology," *The Conflict of Interpretations*, ed. Don Ihde (Evanston, Ill.: Northwestern University Press, 1974), 232–35. Cf. also Heidegger, "Metaphysics as History of Being," *The End of Philosophy*, 46–49, where he distinguishes subjectivity as the logical correlate of objectivity from subjectivity as the *locus* for the "presencing" of Being and then adds: "In its history as metaphysics, Being is through and through subjectity" (ibid., 47). What I mean by *subjectivity* is thus what Heidegger appears to intend with *subjectity*.

4. Plato, *The Republic*, B, 6 (509D–511E), in *The Republic of Plato*, trans. F. M. Cornford (New York: Oxford University Press, 1945), 221–26.

5. W. T. Jones, *A History of Western Philosophy*, vol. 1 [*The Classical Mind*], 2d ed. (New York: Harcourt, Brace & World, 1969), 124.

6. Frederick Copleston, S. J., *A History of Philosophy*, vol. I, part 1 (New York: Doubleday, 1962), 217–18.

7. Aristotle, *Metaphysics*, 1074b, in *The Works of Aristotle*, ed. W. D. Ross, vol. 8, trans. W. D. Ross, 2d ed (Oxford: Clarendon Press, 1928).

8. Ibid., 1072a.

9. Ibid., 1028a.

10. Ibid., 1041b. Cf. also Heidegger, "Metaphysics as History of Being," 8–10. Heidegger believes that Aristotle was more faithful than Plato to the pristine Greek understanding of Being as "presencing"; hence, Aristotle emphasized the priority of the concrete individual existent (which thus comes to presence) over the substantial form (which is its distinctive manner of presencing). At the same time, says Heidegger, Aristotle followed Plato in linking presencing to *eidos* or form. For further comments on this last point, cf. Rorty, *Philosophy and the Mirror of Nature*, 162–63.

11. Sancti Thomae Aquinatis, *Summa Theologiae*, 1, 2, a. 3 (Madrid: Biblioteca de Autores Cristianos, 1951), 18–19.

12. Cf. here Heidegger, "Metaphysics as History of Being," 10–19. Heidegger argues that the Aristotelian *energeia* became in medieval metaphysics *actualitas*. The notion of Being as presencing was thereby effectively lost since *actualitas* was understood in terms of various causal schemes linking God as supreme actuality *(actus purus)* to his creatures. In this respect, as Heidegger comments, physical objects such as plants, animals, or even human beings are akin to mathematical objects (e.g., numbers, ratios); one and all are fixed in their being and intelligibility by a process of "calculation" or "construction" (ibid., 18).

13. René Descartes, *A Discourse on Method*, part 4, trans. John Veitch (London: J. M. Dent, 1965), 26–32. Cf. also Heidegger, "Metaphysics as History of Being," 19–32, where he makes clear that the quest for certitude was likewise characteristic of medieval thought, although it was based on faith in God rather than on the experience of the self in thinking.

14. John Locke, *An Essay Concerning Human Understanding*, introduction, n. 2; ed. A. C. Fraser, 2 vols. (New York: Dover Press, 1959), 1:27. Cf. also Rorty, *Philosophy and the Mirror of Nature*, 139–48. Rorty argues that Locke confuses a hypothetical explanation of the causes of human knowledge with the justification of one's beliefs through reasons or arguments. Granted that there is a legitimate distinction between reasons and causes, it is not clear to me that reasons can be so totally divorced from causes as Rorty seems to demand. One's reasons for making various assertions are inevitably grounded in one's antece-

dent convictions about the nature of reality and the implicit network of causal relations governing one's own and others' experience. Rorty favors the discussion of reasons rather than the analysis of causes because of his antimetaphysical bias, i.e., his conviction that it is fruitless to search for the foundations of human knowledge and activity in any overarching worldview or a priori scheme. Philosophy, in his view, is an ongoing conversation between individuals who exchange more or less satisfactory reasons for their divergent beliefs and corresponding behavior (ibid., 357–94).

15. Cf. James Collins, *A History of Modern European Philosophy* (Milwaukee: Bruce, 1954), 315–17.

16. Ibid., 458–68.

17. Johann Gottlieb Fichte, *Erste Einleitung in die Wissenschaftslehre*, Abschnitt 7, ed. Fritz Medicus (Hamburg: Felix Meiner Verlag, 1961), 30.

18. Ibid., 27.

19. F. W. J. Schelling, *Erster Entwurf eines Systems der Naturphilosophie* (1799); in *Sämtliche Werke*, 14 vols., ed. K. F. A. Schelling (Stuttgart: Cotta Verlag, 1856ff), 3:17–18. N.B.: I follow here the pagination of the original edition of Schelling's collected works, which is given at the top of the page in *Schellings Werke*, ed. Manfred Schröter (Munich: C. H. Beck Verlag, 1958ff).

20. Ibid., 20–33.

21. Hermann Zeltner, "Gleichgewicht als Seinsprinzip, Schellings Philosophie des Gleichgewichts," *Studium Generale* 14 (1961): 498–504.

22. F. W. J. Schelling, *Philosophische Untersuchungen über das Wesen der menschlichen Freiheit* (1809); in *Sämtliche Werke* 7, 357 ff. This work was translated into English by James Gutman under the title *Of Human Freedom* (Chicago: Open Court, 1936).

23. Cf. Collins, *History of Modern European Philosophy*, "Hegel," esp. 608–13; cf. also Quentin Lauer, S.J., *Hegel's Concept of God* (Albany: State University of New York Press, 1982), 128–61.

24. Cf. G. W. F. Hegel, *The Phenomenology of Mind*, trans. J. B. Baillie, 2d ed. (London: George Allen & Unwin, 1955), 67–130, esp. 80–88; 789–808.

25. Cf. Richard J. Bernstein, *Praxis and Action* (Philadelphia: University of Pennsylvania Press, 1971), 11–83, esp. 50–55.

26. David Tracy, *The Analogical Imagination* (New York: Crossroad Press, 1981), 349.

27. This is not to deny, of course, that individuals through a series of "conversions" (intellectual, moral, and religious) can achieve a higher degree of rational self-consciousness than they currently possess (cf. on this point Bernard J. F. Lonergan, S.J., *Insight*, 3d ed. [New York: Philosophical Library, 1970]; likewise by the same author, *Method in Theology*, 2d ed. [New York: Herder & Herder, 1973], esp. 235–93). But it still remains debatable whether the human mind even after these "conversions" consistently attains the kind of objectivity that is simply taken for granted in classical metaphysics (cf. my article, "Authentic Subjectivity and Genuine Objectivity," *Horizons* 11 [1984]: 290–303).

28. Cf. Martin Heidegger, *Identity and Difference*, trans. Joan Stambaugh (New York: Harper & Row, 1969), 54.

29. For a brief summary of the important philosophical issues thus left unresolved by the later Heidegger, cf. Werner Marx, *Heidegger und die Tradition* (Stuttgart: W. Kohlhammer Verlag, 1961), 238–52.

30. Joan Stambaugh, introduction to *The End of Philosophy*, xi.

31. Rorty, *Philosophy and the Mirror of Nature*, 12–13, 38–45.

32. Ibid., 365–72.

33. Jacques Derrida, *Of Grammatology*, trans. G. C. Spivak (Baltimore: Johns Hopkins University Press, 1976), 10.

34. Jacques Derrida, "Freud and the Scene of Writing," *Writing and Difference*, trans. Alan Bass (Chicago: University of Chicago Press, 1978), 196–231; cf. also "Différance," *Margins of Philosophy*, 17–21; cf., finally, Spivak's introduction to *Of Grammatology*, xxxviii–xlv.

35. Derrida, *Writing and Difference*, 280–81.

36. Derrida, "Différance," *Margins of Philosophy*, 11.

37. Cf. on this point Robert Magliola, *Derrida on the Mend* (West Lafayette, Ind.: Purdue University Press, 1984). Magliola tries to integrate Derrida's critique of logocentrism with the mystical tradition of both the East and West. In a future book-length publication, I plan to reinterpret key terms from Derrida's philosophy like "différance," "trace," etc., within the context of the neo-Whiteheadian philosophy set forth in this book. In this way, deconstruction may eventually be seen as an intermediate stage in the reconstruction of metaphysics.

38. Alfred North Whitehead, *Process and Reality*, 167 (254).

39. Ibid., 106–9 (163–67).

40. Ibid., 177–78 (269–70).

41. Ian Barbour, *Myths, Models and Paradigms: A Comparative Study in Science and Religion* (New York: Harper & Row, 1974), 7; cf. also 69, where Barbour indicates similarities and differences in the use of theoretical models in science and in religion.

42. Ibid., 47–48.

43. Whitehead, *Process and Reality*, 4 (6).

44. Ibid., 3 (4).

45. Cf. Alfred North Whitehead, *Science and the Modern World* (New York: Macmillan, 1967), 51.

46. Whitehead, *Process and Reality*, 348 (528).

47. Ibid., 350–51 (532).

48. Ibid., 34 (50–51).

49. Magliola's analysis of the Trinity in part four of *Derrida on the Mend* seems to be moving in the same direction; i.e., even within the Godhead, there is no center as such but "contradictory" relations between the divine persons that paradoxically constitute their triunity as one God (ibid., 144–47).

Chapter 1. Substance-Society-Natural System

1. Cf., e.g., Ivor Leclerc, *The Philosophy of Nature* (Washington, D.C.: Catholic University of America Press, 1986), 4–11; likewise, *The Nature of Physical Existence* (New York: Humanities Press, 1972), 29–37, 349–51.

2. Leclerc, *The Nature of Physical Existence*, 244; likewise, *The Philosophy of Nature*, 85–86.

3. Leclerc, *The Nature of Physical Existence*, 246–47; likewise, *The Philosophy of Nature*, 86.

4. Leclerc, *The Nature of Physical Existence*, 256–60; likewise, *The Philosophy of Nature*, 88–89.

5. Leclerc, *The Nature of Physical Existence*, 267–70; likewise, *The Philosophy of Nature*, 116–17.

6. Leclerc, The Nature of Physical Existence, 295–96, 305–6; likewise, The Philosophy of Nature, 127–29.

7. Werner Marx, The Meaning of Aristotle's Ontology (The Hague: Martinus Nijhoff, 1954), 30–37; Ernst Tugendhat, Ti Kata Tinos (Freiburg i. Br.: Karl Alber Verlag, 1958), 81–102. As Tugendhat argues, the substantial form is not only internally one but a principle of unity (ein vereinheitlichendes Prinzip) for the material elements so that they can "present" themselves as this or that concrete reality (85). He is, to be sure, offering a somewhat Heideggerian understanding of Aristotle on this point.

8. Leclerc, The Nature of Physical Existence, 275–76, 290–91; likewise, The Philosophy of Nature, 118–22, 191–93.

9. Leclerc, The Nature of Physical Existence, 276–83; likewise, The Philosophy of Nature, 166–67.

10. Whitehead, Process and Reality, 58 (91); cf. also 25 (38), 29(44).

11. Alfred North Whitehead, Adventures of Ideas (New York: Macmillan, 1933), 241. Cf. also 226–27.

12. Cf. here William J. Garland, "Whitehead's Theory of Causal Objectification," Process Studies 12 (1982): 180–91; also Nancy Frankenberry, "The Power of the Past," Process Studies 13 (1983): 132–42. For an even stronger defense of the idea that actual entities exercise efficient causality upon their successors, cf. Jorge Luis Nobo, Whitehead's Metaphysics of Extension and Solidarity (Albany: State University of New York Press, 1986), 93–105. Cf., however, Lewis S. Ford, "Efficient Causation: Transition or Concrescence?" a hitherto unpublished paper in which Ford is critical of Nobo's thesis on purely textual grounds.

13. Cf., however, his lectures on Whitehead's philosophy given at the Higher Institute of Philosophy in Leuven, Belgium, in 1983. In these lectures, Leclerc concedes that antecedent actual occasions exercise transeunt causality on their successors even as the subsequent occasions actively prehend these predecessor occasions. Referring to a passage in Whitehead's Adventures of Ideas (New York: Macmillan, 1933), 230, he describes the interaction between antecedent and subsequent occasions as a "conjoint activity" (Whitehead's Philosophy between Rationalism and Empiricism [Leuven: Center for Metaphysics and Philosophy of God, 1984], 51–53). It is regretable that this important revision of his thought on Whitehead was not incorporated into Leclerc's more recently published book, The Philosophy of Nature.

14. Leclerc, The Philosophy of Nature, 120–22.

15. Charles Hartshorne, "The Compound Individual," Philosophical Essays for Alfred North Whitehead, ed. F. S. C. Northrop (New York: Russell & Russell, 1936), 193–210. Cf. also John Cobb, "Overcoming Reductionism," Existence and Actuality: Conversations with Charles Hartshorne, ed. John Cobb and Franklin Gamwell (Chicago: University of Chicago Press, 1984), 149–64. In this essay, Cobb reviews the charge of reductionism in Whitehead's philosophy made by Ivor Leclerc, concedes certain difficulties with Whitehead's position in Process and Reality, but in the end defends Hartshorne's solution to these difficulties (as laid out in the above-mentioned article), as opposed to Leclerc's.

16. Whitehead, Process and Reality, 31 (46).

17. As I see it, this is the insight lacking in Hartshorne's and Cobb's understanding of a "compound individual."

18. Leclerc, The Philosophy of Nature, 128.

19. Whitehead, Process and Reality, 89 (137).

20. Ibid., 90 (138).

21. Ibid., 18 (27).

22. Ibid., 91 (139).

23. Ibid., 92 (140).

24. Whitehead, *Adventures of Ideas*, 262.

25. Whitehead, *Process and Reality*, 103 (157).

26. Cobb, "Overcoming Reductionism," 156.

27. Whitehead, *Adventures of Ideas*, 289.

28. Whitehead, *Process and Reality*, 339 (516).

29. Ibid.

30. Hartshorne, "The Compound Individual," 218–20.

31. Jorge Luis Nobo, *Whitehead's Metaphysics of Extension and Solidarity*, 134–35. Nobo's focus, to be sure, is on the dynamic relationship between the individual actual entity and the universe as a whole, whereas mine is on the relationship between the individual entity and the myriad subsocieties to which it also belongs as part of its membership in the cosmic society of the universe.

32. Ervin Laszlo, *Introduction to Systems Philosophy* (New York: Gordon & Breach, 1972), 30.

33. Ibid., 97–117.

34. Ibid., 25–30.

35. Whitehead, *Process and Reality*, 89–92 (136–41).

36. Laszlo, *Introduction to Systems Philosophy*, 176.

37. Whitehead, *Process and Reality*, 89 (137). Cf. also on this issue of ongoing group identity Ervin Laszlo, *The Systems View of the World: The Natural Philosophy of the New Developments in the Sciences* (New York: George Braziller, 1972), 5–10.

38. Laszlo, *Introduction to Systems Philosophy*, 30.

39. Aristotle, *On Generation and Corruption*, 327b, 23–31, *The Works of Aristotle*, ed. W. D. Ross, vol. 2, part 3, trans. H. H. Joachim (Oxford: Clarendon Press, 1930).

40. Leclerc, *The Nature of Physical Existence*, 327–28; cf. also *The Philosophy of Nature*, 128, 136.

41. Edward Pols, *Meditation on a Prisoner: Towards Understanding Action and Mind* (Carbondale: Southern Illinois University Press, 1975), 1–12.

42. Ibid., 41–42.

43. Ibid., 28–48.

44. Ibid., 69–100, 308–21.

45. Ibid., 319–27; cf. also by the same author, *The Acts of Our Being: A Reflection on Agency and Responsibility* (Amherst: University of Massachusetts Press, 1982), 191–212.

46. See above, n. 7.

47. Pols, *Meditation on a Prisoner*, 174–75.

Chapter 2. Energy-Events and Fields

1. Barbour, *Myths, Models and Paradigms*, 73.

2. Ibid., 77.

3. Whitehead, *Process and Reality*, 157–167 (238–54). For detailed discussion of the subphases referred to above, cf. part three of *Process and Reality*,

219–80 (334–428); likewise, for further analysis of an actual occasion as both subject and superject, ibid, 83–89 (127–36).

4. Ibid., 162–63 (246–48).

5. Ibid., 163 (247). Cf. also by the same author *Adventures of Ideas*, 238: "Energy has recognizable paths through time and space. Energy passes from particular occasion to particular occasion." That this energy is primarily psychic energy or feeling rather than simply physical energy is made clear by the following passage on the next page: "The notion of physical energy, which is at the base of physics, must then be conceived as an abstraction from the complex energy, emotional and purposeful, inherent in the subjective form of the final synthesis in which each occasion completes itself."

6. Whitehead, *Process and Reality*, 163 (247).

7. Whitehead, *Science and the Modern World*, 35.

8. Whitehead, *Process and Reality*, 166 (251–52). Cf. also 219–22 (334–40).

9. Ibid., 219–20 (336).

10. Ibid., 65–67 (101–5), 96–97 (147–48). Cf. here Henry P. Stapp, "Einstein Time and Process Time," *Physics and the Ultimate Significance of Time*, ed. David Ray Griffin (Albany: State University of New York Press, 1986), 267–68; also, in the same volume, David Bohm, "Comments on Henry Stapp's 'Einstein Time and Process Time,'" 289–90, and Peter Miller, "On 'Becoming' as a Fifth Dimension," 291–92, for an interesting discussion of the notion of simultaneity within "process time."

11. Ibid., 84 (129).

12. Ibid., 35 (53). Cf. also Abner Shimony, "Quantum Physics and the Philosophy of Whitehead," *Boston Studies in the Philosophy of Science*, vol. 2, ed. Robert S. Cohen and Marx W. Wartofsky (New York: Humanities Press, 1965), 322–30. Shimony argues that, while orthodox Whiteheadianism for various reasons is not compatible with current theories in quantum physics, a new philosophical system combining basic insights from Whitehead and empirical data from the natural sciences is certainly conceivable. In that same line, he proposes that Ultimate Reality within this new scheme "might be some kind of 'field' of diffused primitive feeling, of which the actual occasions are 'quanta' existing whenever there are individual loci of feeling" (324).

13. Karl R. Popper, *Quantum Theory and the Schism in Physics* (Totowa, N.J.: Rowman and Littlefield, 1982), 173–77.

14. Ibid., 195.

15. Ibid., 198.

16. Ibid., 80.

17. Ibid., 81–82.

18. Cf. here Rupert Sheldrake, *A New Science of Life: The Hypothesis of Formative Causation* (Los Angeles: J. P. Tarcher, 1981), 82–85, 114–15, 115–18. This controversial book about the nature of "morphogenetic fields" confirms in many respects my own hypothesis about the function of Whiteheadian societies as fields for successive generations of actual entities. Cf. also John Haught, *The Cosmic Adventure: Science, Religion and the Quest for Purpose* (New York: Paulist Press, 1984), 61–66.

19. Stapp, "Einstein Time and Process Time," 267. For a summary of the differences between Stapp and Whitehead on the issue of simultaneity within "process time," cf. Stapp, "Mind, Matter, and Quantum Mechanics," *Foundations of Physics* 12 (1982): 381–83.

20. Heinz R. Pagels, *The Cosmic Code: Quantum Physics as the Language of Nature* (New York: Bantam Books, 1982), 68.

21. Whitehead, *Process and Reality*, 18 (27).
22. Ibid., 251 (383). Cf. also Whitehead, *Science and the Modern World*, 110.
23. Cf. here Murray Code, *Order and Organism: Steps to a Whiteheadian Philosophy of Mathematics and the Natural Sciences* (Albany: State University of New York Press, 1985), 155–56: "The factor of necessity in any natural law depends upon the continued existence of the defining characteristic of a certain type of society. But this characteristic is an ideal, and an ideal need not always be completely obeyed in the actual processes of the formation of the nexus of a society. There is always an element of disorder linked to any element of actual order."
24. Whitehead, *Process and Reality*, 251–53 (384–87).
25. Ibid., 318 (484).
26. Ibid., 78 (120–21). Cf. also Whitehead, *Science and the Modern World*, 17.
27. Code, *Order and Organism*, 12–13; cf. also 86–87.
28. Ibid., 80–111. Code argues that science produces "homeotypal" explanations of reality, i.e., detailed analyses of different levels of activity within nature, but cannot readily produce without outside assistance "heterotypal" explanations that integrate a number of levels in virtue of a "co-ordinating analogy" drawn from ordinary experience. Yet, only in virtue of such a coordinating analogy can scientists themselves and, even more so, the lay public appreciate the full scope and significance of the "story" that is unfolding piecemeal in different scientific disciplines. One such coordinating analogy, in Code's judgment, is Whitehead's notion of organism, which with proper qualifications applies not only to actual entities but also to all the societies, both animate and inanimate, that the latter at any moment co-constitute.
29. Whitehead, *Process and Reality*, 90 (138).
30. *Ibid.* N.B.: Here is where the philosophical implications of Rupert Sheldrake's theory of "morphogenetic fields" seem to correlate quite readily with Whitehead's philosophy and vice versa. Cf., however, Sheldrake, *A New Science of Life*, 59, where he critiques Whitehead for deriving the forms of things from "Platonic Eternal Objects" rather than from morphogenetic fields. In reply, one could say that the forms are indeed derived from eternal objects in Whitehead's scheme but transmitted from one generation of actual entities to another through the pertinent societies or fields.
31. Whitehead, *Process and Reality*, 90–91 (139).
32. Ibid., 97–98 (148–50).
33. Cf. my book, *The Triune Symbol: Persons, Process and Community* (Lanham, Md.: University Press of America, 1985), 15–31, esp. 20ff. In this book, I describe communities as social processes. But as I make clear in a postscript (189), I belatedly came to the conclusion that processes themselves have to be further specified as fields of activity for the dynamic interrelation of their constituent members.
34. Whitehead, *Process and Reality*, 101–2 (154–55).
35. Ibid., 103 (157).
36. Ibid., 339 (516).
37. Ibid., 90 (138).
38. Cf. here James E. Lindsay, Jr., "The Misapprehension of Presentational Immediacy," *Process Studies* 14 (1985): 145–57.

Chapter 3. Entropy and Dissipative Structures

1. Ilya Prigogine and Isabelle Stengers, *Order out of Chaos: Man's New Dialogue with Nature* (New York: Bantom Books, 1984).
2. Whitehead, *Science and the Modern World*, 29–31.
3. Ibid., 51, 58.
4. Ibid., 58.
5. Ibid., 75–88; 139–56.
6. Ibid., 79–80.
7. Prigogine and Stengers, *Order out of Chaos*, 61.
8. Ibid., 6.
9. Ibid., 6–7; also 30–36.
10. Ibid., 176.
11. *Ibid.*, 180–81.
12. Whitehead, *Process and Reality*, 100 (153).
13. Ibid., 101 (154).
14. Cf. above, chapter 2, for an earlier discussion of the common element of form as grounded in a statistical average for the constituent actual occasions of a society.
15. Whitehead, *Process and Reality*, 102 (155).
16. Prigogine and Stengers, *Order out of Chaos*, 187.
17. Whitehead, *Process and Reality*, 103 (157).
18. Ibid., 107 (163).
19. Ibid., 34–35 (51–52).
20. Ibid., 107 (163–64).
21. Ibid., 339 (516).
22. Ibid., 107–8 (164).
23. Ibid., 101–2 (154–55).
24. Cf. here Joseph E. Earley, "Self-Organization and Agency: In Chemistry and in Process Philosophy," *Process Studies* 11 (1981): 242–58. Earley uses basically the same scientific data with respect to the existence and operation of dissipative structures to argue for an extension of the Whiteheadian notion of actual entity so as to account for these higher-level unities in the fields of chemistry and biology. While dissipative structures, in other words, are clearly "compound individuals . . . made up of components which are, in some sense, also individuals" (242), they are akin to actual entities in that they are unitary sources of effective action (253). While fully agreeing with Earley in his overall conclusion here, I would nevertheless urge once again what I have argued throughout this book, namely, that Whiteheadian societies are functioning ontological unities in their own right, quite irrespective of whether they are governed by a "regnant" subsociety or not (cf. on this point chapter 1). Thus the unity of a dissipative structure in chemistry or biology, in my judgment, is not the unity of an actual entity (as Earley proposes), but the unity of a society.
25. Prigogine and Stengers, *Order out of Chaos*, 189.
26. Whitehead, *Process and Reality*, 100 (153). Cf. also *Science and the Modern World*, 107–12.
27. Cf. here David Ray Griffin, "Bohm and Whitehead on Wholeness, Freedom, Causality and Time," *Physics and the Ultimate Significance of Time*, 142–43.

28. Prigogine and Stengers, *Order out of Chaos*, 251.
29. Ibid., 260.
30. Ibid., 285.
31. Ibid.

Chapter 4. Subjective Spirit: The Power of Radical Self-Determination

1. Martin Heidegger, *Schellings Abhandlung über das Wesen der menschlichen Freiheit*, ed. Hildegard Feick (Tübingen: Max Niemeyer Verlag, 1971), 4.

2. For my analysis of Heidegger's lectures I am much indebted to Michael Vater's article some years ago: "Heidegger and Schelling: The Finitude of Being," *Idealistic Studies* 5 (1975): 20–58.

3. Ibid., 23–34; also Heidegger, *Schellings Abhandlung*, 58–74.

4. F. W. J. Schelling, *Sämtliche Werke*; 7:340–47.

5. Heidegger, *Schellings Abhandlung*, 105.

6. Schelling, *Werke*, 7:352.

7. Vater, "Heidegger and Schelling," 22; cf. also 41–50.

8. Heidegger, *Schellings Abhandlung*, 183–88; cf. also Schelling, *Werke*, 7:382–89.

9. Heidegger, *Schellings Abhandlung*, 186.

10. Ibid., 188–91, 195–96.

11. Ibid., 194; cf. also Vater, "Heidegger and Schelling," 50–58.

12. Hermann Zeltner, "Gleichgewicht als Seinsprinzip: Schellings Philosophie des Gleichgewichts," *Studium Generale* 14 (1961): 495–508, esp. 504–5. Cf. also Antoon Braeckman, "Whitehead and German Idealism: A Poetic Heritage," *Process Studies* 14 (1984–85): 281. He, too, confirms the existence and operation of a *Gleichgewichtsprinzip* in Schelling's philosophy.

13. Joseph A. Bracken, *Freiheit und Kausalität bei Schelling* [*Symposion*, n. 38] (Freiburg i. Br.: Alber Verlag, 1972).

14. Schelling, *Werke*, 7:364.

15. Ibid., 389–94.

16. Cf. here Heidegger, *Schellings Abhandlung*, 128–35; likewise, Vater, "Heidegger and Schelling," 50–58.

17. Cf. Immanuel Kant, *Critique of Pure Reason*, trans. Norman Kemp Smith (New York: St. Martin's Press, 1965), 152–58 (B 130–40). Kant himself refers to this synthesizing activity of the understanding as "an act of the self-activity of the subject . . . [that] cannot be executed save by the subject itself" (152 [B 130]).

18. Schelling, *Werke* 7:383–88.

19. The term *Abgrund* is actually used by Schelling only with respect to the primitive undifferentiated unity of divine consciousness. But, from other texts in *Of Human Freedom*, it is clear that the equivalent of an *Abgrund* is likewise present in human consciousnesness (cf., e.g. *Werke* 7:363). In fact, as I try to make clear in my book on Schelling, the model for the operation of divine consciousness is patently Schelling's analysis of human consciousness (cf. here *Freiheit und Kausalität bei Schelling*, 47).

20. Schelling, *Werke* 7:352.

21. Heidegger, *Schellings Abhandlung*, 186; cf. also 185; "Das Eigenwesen jedes Menschen . . ."

22. Schelling, *Werke*, 7:433.

23. F. W. J. Schelling, *Die Weltalter. Fragmente*, ed. Manfred Schröter (Munich: Biederstein & Leibniz, 1946), 2:23.

24. Wolfgang Wieland, *Schellings Lehre von der Zeit* (Heidelberg: Winter Verlag, 1956), 39.

25. Ibid., 42.

26. Martin Heidegger, *Being and Time*, trans. John Macquarrie & Edward Robinson (New York: Harper & Row, 1962), 344–45.

27. Martin Heidegger, *Kant and the Problem of Metaphysics*, trans. James Churchill (Bloomington: Indiana University Press, 1968), 93–129.

28. Martin Heidegger, *Vom Wesen des Grundes* (Frankfurt a. M.: Klostermann Verlag, 1955), 43.

29. Ibid., 53.

30. Wieland, *Schellings Lehre*, 30.

31. Ibid., 37–42.

32. Ibid., 42.

33. Ibid., 69–70.

34. Whitehead, *Process and Reality*, 88 (135). Cf. also Braeckman, "Whitehead and German Idealism," 278–79, where he argues that for both Schelling and Whitehead the ultimate ground of Being is not an entity, but rather an underlying ontological activity.

35. Wolfhart Pannenberg, *Anthropology in Theological Perspective*, trans. Matthew O'Connell (Philadelphia: Westminster, 1985), 201.

36. Johann Gottlieb Fichte, *Science of Knowledge*, trans. Peter Heath & John Lachs (New York: Appleton-Century-Crofts, 1970), 93–102.

37. Pannenberg, *Anthropology*, 203.

38. Ibid., 221.

39. Whitehead, *Process and Reality*, 85 (130).

40. Pannenberg, *Anthropology*, 222.

41. Cf. here Wolfhart Pannenberg, "Atom, Duration, Form: Difficulties with Process Philosophy," *Process Studies* 14 (1984): 26–27. Pannenberg sides with William James in affirming that the successive moments of human consciousness are really distinct because of the complexity of operations therein involved at each moment. Yet, paradoxically, he also labels Whitehead's doctrine of actual occasions "atomistic" because of an alleged lack of continuity between successive occasions. At least as I see it, Whitehead's actual occasions, which are in no way self-conscious but only conscious of their derivation from the self, are less "atomistic" than the discrete moments of experience attributed to the ego by Pannenberg and James.

42. Pannenberg, *Anthropology*, 240.

43. Whitehead, *Process and Reality*, 161 (244); cf. also 350 (531).

44. Ibid., 163 (247): "In the phraseology of physics . . ."

45. See below, chapter 7, where I discuss how human temporal consciousness should be understood as a structured field of activity for its successive occasions.

46. Cf. Pannenberg, "Atom, Duration, Form," pp. 28–29. Here he proposes that Whitehead's notion of "subjective aim" and "superject" be recast so as to be made more consistent with his own understanding of causality as future-oriented and future-determined. Others have pointed out, however, that Pan-

nenberg's own thinking on this issue remains somewhat ambiguous (cf., e.g., Philip Clayton, "The God of History and the Presence of the Future," *Journal of Religion* 65 [1985]: 105–8). For he rejects the traditional Aristotelian notion of final causality as something already predetermined (at least, in principle), but does not seem to offer a clear alternative. Perhaps some of his difficulties could be resolved by adopting the neo-Whiteheadian notion of society advocated in this book: namely, that a society is an ongoing field of activity for successive generations of actual entities but with an emergent entelechy or teleological orientation of its own. That is, its structure or "common element of form" undergoes change or development in a given direction as it is transmitted from one generation of actual occasions to another within the society or field of activity. Only in this way, as I see it, is the presently concrescing occasion genuinely free to become itself; that is, it is conditioned by both the past and the anticipated future of the society to which it belongs, but determined by neither of them.

Chapter 5. Objective Spirit: Structured Fields of Activity

1. Collins, *History of Modern European Philosophy*, 643.
2. G. W. F. Hegel, *Hegel's Philosophy of Mind* (*Encyclopedia of the Philosophical Sciences*, part 3), trans. William Wallace (Oxford: Clarendon Press, 1971), n. 377 *Zusatz*.
3. Ibid., n. 384 *Zusatz*.
4. G. W. F. Hegel, *Hegel's Philosophy of Nature* (*Encyclopedia of the Philosophical Sciences*, part 2), trans. A. V. Miller (Oxford: Clarendon press, 1970), n. 254.
5. Ibid., n. 261 *Zusatz*.
6. Ibid., n. 247 *Zusatz*.
7. Ibid., n. 285.
8. Ibid., n. 341.
9. Hegel, *The Phenomenology of Mind*, 81. N.B.: I have slightly modified Baillie's translation here.
10. Ibid., 82. Cf. also Collins, *History of Modern European Philosophy*, 623–24.
11. Whitehead, *Process and Reality*, 89 (137).
12. Ibid., 18 (27).
13. Pannenberg, "Atom, Duration, Form," 27.
14. Whitehead, *Process and Reality*, 35 (53).
15. Ibid., 34 (51).
16. Ibid., 107 (163).
17. Ibid., 178 (270).
18. Hegel, *Philosophy of Mind*, n. 535.
19. G. W. F. Hegel, *The Philosophy of Right* (*Great Books of the Western World*, n. 46), trans. T. M. Knox (Chicago: Encyclopedia Britannica, 1955), n. 257.
20. Cf. here Paul Lakeland, *The Politics of Salvation: The Hegelian Idea of the State* (Albany: State University of New York Press, 1984), 57: "Through activity done in accordance with the true nature of human beings, the state is present in the world. And the idea of the state as the ethical substance is the idea of a community in which all actions are done in accordance with the truth

of human nature, and thus a truly free, absolutely rational community is present in history." Lakeland concedes, of course, that this ideal state has never been concretely realized in human history.

21. Hegel, Philosophy of Mind, n. 279, Addition (Zusatz).
22. Ibid., n. 272.
23. Ibid., n. 280, Addition (Zusatz).
24. Ibid., n. 298.
25. Whitehead, Adventures of Ideas, 86.
26. Ibid., 71, 80–81.
27. Ibid., 39–40.
28. David L. Hall, The Civilization of Experience: A Whiteheadian Theory of Culture (New York: Fordham University Press, 1973), 69.
29. Lakeland argues that Hegel's ideal state is not "totalitarian or monolithic" because the rational will of the state is only actualized in and through the will of individual human beings acting in concert (cf. Lakeland, The Politics of Salvation, 21). While this is certainly true in theory, the notion of a sovereign rational will of the state remains suspect because, as Lakeland himself admits (cf. above, note 20), no group of human beings has ever succeeded in creating and sustaining a fully rational social order.
30. Whitehead, Process and Reality, 31 (46).

Chapter 6. The Triune God

1. Cf. above, foreword.
2. Bracken, The Triune Symbol, 44.
3. The names of the first two divine persons are written in quotation marks here and elsewhere to indicate their purely metaphorical, nonsexist use.
4. In a journal article some years ago, I indicated how this process-oriented understanding of the doctrine of the Trinity is actually quite similar to Thomas Aquinas's exposition of the doctrine of the Trinity in the Summa Theologiae, 1, 29, a. 4 corpus (cf. "Subsistent Relation: Mediating Concept for a New Synthesis?" Journal of Religion 64 [1984]: 188–204). For therein Aquinas describes the divine persons as subsistent relations that share one and the same divine being in relatively different ways. That is, the "Father" is God precisely as "Father"; the "Son" is the same God as "Son"; the Spirit, as Spirit. Aquinas and his followers, however, understood these "relations" as fixed entities (nouns) rather than as ongoing activities (verbs). From a process-oriented perspective, however, the first divine person is not "Father" so much as "Father-ing," the activity of initiating a dialogue with the divine "Son." Similarly, the second person is less the "Son" than the ongoing activity of "Son-ing," i.e., continually responding to the originating activity of the "Father." Finally, the third divine person is not so much the entity called Spirit as rather the activity of Spirit-ing, i.e., empowering the "Father" to offer and the "Son" to respond. As I indicated in the article, Aquinas with the doctrine of the divine persons as subsistent relations was on the verge of a process-relational understanding of reality that would stand in sharp contrast with the relatively static, substance-oriented approach to Being characteristic of Aristotle and his successors up to the time of Aquinas. But Aquinas confined the notion of subsistent relation to the divine persons and even there, as noted above, conceived relation more as an entity than as an activity.
5. Whitehead, Process and Reality, 349–51 (530–32).

6. Bracken, *The Triune Symbol*, 38, 46.

7. That it was the "Son" who according to Christian belief became incarnate in Jesus of Nazareth and served as Redeemer of the human race in its struggle for reconciliation with the Father is a topic that I discuss at length in *The Triune Symbol* but will not deal with here (cf. *The Triune Symbol*, 48–57, 69–81). For, even apart from an incarnation in Jesus of Nazareth, the "Son" is according to this scheme the implicit focal point of creation as a semiautonomous reality within the communitarian life of the three divine persons.

8. Cf. here Nobo, *Whitehead's Metaphysics of Extension and Solidarity*, 267–73.

9. Whitehead, *Process and Reality*, 21 (31).

10. Ibid., 88 (135).

11. Bracken, *The Triune Symbol*, 45–47.

12. Ibid., 45.

13. Ibid., 46.

14. Whitehead, *Process and Reality*, 67 (104–5), 215 (327).

15. Ibid., 46 (73).

16. Ibid., 161 (244). Whitehead is making reference here to human beings in their temporal consciousness; but, *a fortiori*, this would apply to the consciousness of each of the divine persons. Cf. also below, chapter 7, where I discuss how the divine persons and all finite occasions within the divine communitarian life prehend the subjectivity of their predecessor occasions in and through objectifications in the field.

17. Ibid., 66 (103).

18. Cf. Nobo, *Whitehead's Metaphysics of Extension and Solidarity*, 205–49. One of Nobo's key contentions is that the extensive continuum is eternal and unchanging whereas the space-time continuum is constantly being altered by reason of the patterns established by successive generations of occasions.

19. Ibid., 207.

20. Ibid., 256.

21. Ibid., 109.

22. Whitehead, *Science and the Modern World*, 105.

23. Ibid., 179.

24. Whitehead, *Process and Reality*, 348 (528): "God and the World are the contrasted opposites in terms of which Creativity achieves its supreme task of transforming disjoined multiplicity, with its diversities in opposition, into concrescent unity, with its diversities in contrast."

25. Bracken, *The Triune Symbol*, 44.

26. Whitehead, *Process and Reality*, 88 (135).

27. Ibid., 348 (528).

28. Ibid., 340 (517).

29. Ibid., 346 (525).

30. Ibid., 338 (514).

31. Ibid., 350–51 (532).

32. This is not to deny, of course, that finite entities retain their individual identity within God (cf. on this point Whitehead, *Process and Reality*, 350–51 [532], cited above). But, even so, they remain accidental modifications of one substantial reality. Otherwise, Whitehead would be implicitly endorsing my own view of Ultimate Reality as a cosmic society.

33. Charles Hartshorne, *The Divine Relativity: A Social Conception of God* (New Haven: Yale University Press, 1964), 89.

34. Cf., e.g., Charles Hartshorne, *Man's Vision of God and the Logic of Theism* (Hamden, Conn.: Archon Books, 1964), 174–211.

35. Ibid., 198.

36. Cf. Hartshorne, "The Compound Individual," 218–20.

Chapter 7. The Cosmic Society

1. Cf. Edward Conze, *Buddhism: Its Essence and Development* (New York: Harper Torchbook, 1975), 152–59.

2. Whitehead, *Process and Reality*, 161 (244): "We—as enduring objects with personal order—objectify the occasions of our own past with peculiar completeness in our immediate present." Whitehead, to be sure, does not thereby say that past occasions are prehended in their subjective immediacy by their successors. This is a further inference on my part, grounded in the experience of identifying with my own previous conscious states. See also on this point John B. Cobb, Jr., *A Christian Natural Theology* (Philadelphia: Westminster Press, 1965), 74–79. Cobb argues that, in prehending primarily the mental pole of their predecessors, the occasions constitutive of human temporal consciousness identify with them as their own previous experiences, i.e., as I see it, identify with them in their subjective immediacy.

3. Whitehead, *Process and Reality*, 347 (527).

4. Ibid., 350–51 (532).

5. Ibid., 85 (130).

6. David Griffin, "The Possibility of Subjective Immortality in Whitehead's Philosophy," *The Modern Schoolman* 53 (1975–76): 56. N.B.: Griffin seems to be making much the same argument with respect to the occasions constituting the human psyche that I advanced above for all occasions whatsoever upon incorporation into the communitarian life of the three divine persons. That is, once freed from the constraints of existence in the space-time continuum, the occasion is able to prehend its predecessors not simply as objects, but in their subjective immediacy. I will return to this theme below.

7. Marjorie Suchocki, *The End of Evil: Process Eschatology in Historical Context* (Albany: State University of New York Press, 1988), 88.

8. Whitehead, *Process and Reality*, 41 (66).

9. Suchocki, *The End of Evil*, 91.

10. Ibid., 106.

11. Ibid., 109.

12. Charles Hartshorne, *The Logic of Perfection and Other Essays in Neoclassical Metaphysics* (LaSalle, Ill.: Open Court, 1962), 261.

13. Ibid., 254.

14. Suchocki, *The End of Evil*, 103, 112. See also on this point J. Norman King and Barry L. Whitney, "Rahner and Hartshorne on Death and Eternal Life," *Horizons* 15 (1988): 254.

15. Suchocki, *The End of Evil*, 111.

16. Ibid.

17. Suchocki, moreover, makes clear in other passages her belief that the neo-Whiteheadian eschatology sketched in her book represents a doctrine of universal salvation. Cf., e.g., 113, 170–71.

18. Whitehead, *Process and Reality*, 347 (527). Italics mine.

19. Suchocki, *The End of Evil*, 133.

20. Whitehead, *Process and Reality*, 90 (138).

21. Suchocki, *The End of Evil*, 95.

22. Cf. above, introduction.

23. Bernard Meland, *Fallible Forms and Symbols: Discourses on Method in a Theology of Culture* (Philadelphia: Fortress Press, 1976), 151–52.

24. Cf. on this point Frankenberry, *Religion and Radical Empiricism*, 135.

25. Whitehead, *Process and Reality*, 348 (528).

26. Whitehead, *Science and the Modern World*, 179.

27. Bernard M. Loomer, "The Size of God," in *The Size of God: The Theology of Bernard Loomer in Context*, ed. William Dean and Larry E. Axel (Macon, GA: Mercer Univ. Press, 1987), 41.

28. John B. Cobb, Jr., "Response to Loomer," *The Size of God*, 53.

29. Loomer, "The Size of God," 42.

30. Ibid., 51.

31. Cf. on this point Bernard J. Lee, "Loomer on Deity: A Long Night's Journey into Day," *The Size of God*, 75. See also below, the appendix.

32. Loomer, "The Size of God," 20; cf.also 42–50.

33. Cf. here William A. Christian, *An Interpretation of Whitehead's Metaphysics* (New Haven: Yale University Press, 1959), 327–30. Christian likewise argues that past occasions are "given" for prehension by presently concrescing occasions in God; but he contends that they are given only as objectively prehended by God and thus as totally conformed to the divine subjective aim.

34. Loomer, "The Size of God," 51.

35. Suchocki, *The End of Evil*, 110.

36. Whitehead, *Adventures of Ideas*, 367.

Appendix

1. Sir Julian Huxley, introduction to *The Phenomenon of Man* by Pierre Teilhard de Chardin, trans. Bernard Wall (New York: Harper & Row, 1959), 11.

2. Toulmin, *Return to Cosmology*, 113–26, esp. 125–26.

3. Teilhard, *Phenomenon of Man*, 269: "A present and real noosphere [sphere of mind proper to human evolution] goes with a real and present centre. To be supremely attractive, Omega must be supremely present." Cf. also Christopher F. Mooney, S.J., *Teilhard de Chardin and the Mystery of Christ* (New York: Harper & Row, 1966), 176–77. The process of Christogenesis began with creation, received its definitive directionality in the incarnation of the Son of God in Jesus of Nazareth, and continues in the struggle of human beings for ever more comprehensive forms of life in community.

4. Whitehead, *Process and Reality*, 100–1 (153–54).

5. Whitehead, *Process and Reality*, 21 (31); Teilhard, *Phenomenon of Man*, 40–43. Cf. also on this point Bernard Lee, *The Becoming of the Church* (New York: Paulist Press, 1974), 121–53, esp. 127.

6. Teilhard, *Phenomenon of Man*, 40; Whitehead, *Process and Reality*, 18 (27–28).

7. James Fredericks, S.S., "The Kyoto School: Modern Buddhist Philosophy and the Search for a Transcultural Theology," *Horizons* 15 (1988): 299–315.

8. Keiji Nishitani, *Religion and Nothingness*, trans. Jan Van Bragt (Berkeley: University of California Press, 1982), 150–51.

9. Ibid., 90, 106.

10. Ibid., 123: Absolute Emptiness "is at bottom one with being, even as being is at bottom one with emptiness."

11. Ibid., 61–62.

Select Bibliography

Books

Aquinatis, Sancti Thomae. *Summa Theologiae*. Madrid: Biblioteca de Autores Cristianos, 1951.

Aristotle, *Metaphysics*. In *The Works of Aristotle*. Edited by W. D. Ross. Vol. 8. Translated by W. D. Ross. 2d ed. Oxford: Clarendon Press, 1928.

———. *On Generation and Corruption: The Works of Aristotle*. Edited by W. D. Ross. Vol. 2, part 3. Translated by H. H. Joachim. Oxford: Clarendon Press, 1930.

Barbour, Ian. *Myths, Models and Paradigms: A Comparative Study in Science and Religion*. New York: Harper & Row, 1974.

Bernstein, Richard J. *Praxis and Action*. Philadelphia: University of Pennsylvania Press, 1971.

Bracken, Joseph A. *Freiheit und Kausalität bei Schelling (Symposion*, n. 38). Freiburg i. Br.: Alber Verlag, 1972.

———. *The Triune Symbol: Persons, Process and Community*. Lanham, Md: University Press of America, 1985.

Christian, William A. *An Interpretation of Whitehead's Metaphysics*. New Haven: Yale University Press, 1959.

Cobb, John B., Jr. *A Christian Natural Theology*. Philadelphia: Westminster Press, 1965.

Code, Murray. *Order and Organism: Steps to a Whiteheadian Philosophy of Mathematics and the Natural Sciences*. Albany: State University of New York Press, 1985.

Collins, James. *A History of Modern European Philosophy*. Milwaukee: Bruce, 1954.

Conze, Edward. *Buddhism: Its Essence and Development*. New York: Harper Torchbook, 1975.

Copleston, Frederick, S. J. *A History of Philosophy*. Vol. 1, part 1. New York: Doubleday, 1962.

Derrida, Jacques. *Margins of Philosophy*. Translated by Alan Bass. Chicago: University of Chicago Press, 1982.

———. *Of Grammatology*. Translated by G. C. Spivak. Baltimore: Johns Hopkins University Press, 1976.

———. *Writing and Difference*. Translated by Alan Bass. Chicago: University of Chicago Press, 1978.

Descartes, René. *A Discourse on Method*. Translated by John Veitch. London: J. M. Dent, 1965.

Fichte, Johann Gottlieb. *Erste Einleitung in die Wissenschaftslehre*. Edited by Fritz Medicus. Hamburg: Felix Meiner Verlag, 1961.

———. *Science of Knowledge*. Translated by Peter Heath and John Lachs. New York: Appleton-Century-Crofts, 1970.

Frankenberry, Nancy. *Religion and Radical Empiricism*. Albany: State University of New York Press, 1987.

Hall, David L. *The Civilization of Experience: A Whiteheadian Theory of Culture*. New York: Fordham University Press, 1973.

Hartshorne, Charles. *The Divine Relativity: A Social Conception of God*. New Haven: Yale University Press, 1964.

———. *The Logic of Perfection and Other Essays in Neoclassical Metaphysics*. La Salle, Ill.: Open Court, 1962.

———. *Man's Vision of God and the Logic of Theism*. Hamden, Conn.: Archon Books, 1964.

Haught, John. *The Cosmic Adventure: Science, Religion and the Quest for Purpose*. New York: Paulist Press, 1984.

Hegel, G. W. F. *Hegel's Philosophy of Mind*. Encyclopedia of the Philosophical Sciences, part 3. Translated by William Wallace. Oxford: Clarendon Press, 1971.

———. *Hegel's Philosophy of Nature*. Encyclopedia of the Philosophical Sciences, part 2). Translated by A. V. Miller. Oxford: Clarendon Press, 1970.

———. *The Phenomenology of Mind*. Translated by J. B. Baillie. 2d ed. London: George Allen and Unwin, 1955.

———. *The Philosophy of Right*. Great Books of the Western World, n. 46. Translated by T. M. Knox. Chicago: Encyclopedia Britannica, 1955.

Heidegger, Martin. *Being and Time*. Translated by John Macquarrie and Edward Robinson, New York: Harper & Row, 1962.

———. *Kant and the Problem of Metaphysics*. Translated by James Churchill. Bloomington: Indiana University Press, 1968.

———. *Identity and Difference*. Translated by Joan Stambaugh. New York: Harper & Row, 1969.

———. *The End of Philosophy*. Translated by Joan Stambaugh. New York: Harper & Row, 1973.

———. *Holzwege*. 6th ed. Frankfurt am M.: Vittorio Klostermann, 1980.

———. *Vom Wesen des Grundes*. Frankfurt am M.: Klostermann Verlag, 1955.

Jones. W. T. *A History of Western Philosophy*. 4 Vols. 2d ed. New York: Harcourt, Brace and World, 1969.

Kant, Immanuel. *Critique of Pure Reason*. Translated by Norman Kemp Smith. New York: St. Martin's Press, 1965.

Laszlo, Ervin. *Introduction to Systems Philosophy*. New York: Gordon and Breach, 1972.

———. *The Systems View of the World: The Natural Philosophy of the New Developments in the Sciences*. New York: Braziller, 1972.

Lauer, Quentin, S. J. *Hegel's Concept of God*. Albany: State University of New York Press, 1982.

Leclerc, Ivor. *The Nature of Physical Existence*. New York: Humanities Press, 1972.

————. *The Philosophy of Nature*. Washington, D.C.: Catholic University of America Press, 1986.

Lee, Bernard, S. M. *The Becoming of the Church: A Process Theology of the Structures of Christian Experience*. New York: Paulist Press, 1974.

Locke, John. *An Essay Concerning Human Understanding*. Edited by A. C. Fraser. 2 vols. New York: Dover Press, 1959.

Lonergan, Bernard J. F., S. J. *Insight*. 3d ed. New York: Philosophical Library, 1970.

————. *Method in Theology*. 2d ed. New York: Herder and Herder, 1973.

Magliola, Robert. *Derrida on the Mend*. West Lafayette, Ind.: Purdue University Press, 1984.

Marx, Werner. *Heidegger und die Tradition*. Stuttgart: W. Kohlhammer Verlag, 1961.

————. *The Meaning of Aristotle's Ontology*. The Hague: Martinus Nijhoff, 1954.

Meland, Bernard. *Fallible Forms and Symbols: Discourses on Method in a Theology of Culture*. Philadelphia: Fortress Press, 1976.

New Encyclopedia of Philosophy. Edited by J. Grooten and G. Jo Steenbergen. Translated by E. van den Bossche. New York: Philosophical Library, 1972.

Nishitani, Keiji. *Religion and Nothingness*. Translated with an introduction by Jan Van Bragt. Berkeley: University of California Press, 1982.

Nobo, Jorge Luis. *Whitehead's Metaphysics of Extension and Solidarity*. Albany: State University of New York Press, 1986.

Pagels, Heinz. *The Cosmic Code: Quantum Physics as the Language of Nature*. New York: Bantam Books, 1982.

Pannenberg, Wolfhart. *Anthropology in Theological Perspective*. Translated by Matthew O'Connell. Philadelphia: Westminster Press, 1985.

Plato. *The Republic*. Translated by F. M. Cornford. New York: Oxford University Press, 1945.

Pols, Edward. *The Acts of Our Being: A Reflection on Agency and Responsibility*. Amherst: University of Massachusetts Press, 1982.

————. *Meditation on a Prisoner: Towards Understanding Action and Mind*. Carbondale: Southern Illinois University Press, 1975.

Popper, Karl. *Quantum Theory and the Schism in Physics*. Totowa, N.J.: Rowman and Littlefield, 1982.

Prigogine, Ilya, and Isabelle Stengers. *Order out of Chaos: Man's New Dialogue with Nature*. New York: Bantam Books, 1984.

Ricoeur, Paul. *The Conflict of Interpretations*. Edited by Don Ihde. Evanston, Ill.: Northwestern University Press, 1974.

Rorty, Richard. *Philosophy and the Mirror of Nature*. Princeton: Princeton University Press, 1979.

Schelling, F. W. J. *Die Weltalter. Fragmente*. Edited by Manfred Schröter. Munich: Biederstein and Leibniz, 1946.

————. *Sämtliche Werke*. 14 Vols. Edited by K. F. A. Schelling. Stuttgart: Cotta Verlag, 1856ff. In *Schellings Werke*. Edited by Manfred Schröter. Munich: C. H. Beck Verlag, 1958ff.

Sheldrake, Rupert. *A New Science of Life: The Hypothesis of Formative Causation.* Los Angeles: J. P. Tarcher, 1981.

Suchocki, Marjorie. *The End of Evil: Process Eschatology in Historical Context.* Albany: State University of New York Press, 1988.

Teilhard de Chardin, Pierre. *The Phenomenon of Man.* Translated by Bernard Wall. New York: Harper & Row, 1959.

Toulmin, Stephen. *The Return to Cosmology: Post Modern Science and the Theology of Nature.* Berkeley: University of California Press, 1985.

Tracy, David. *The Analogical Imagination.* New York: Crossroad Press, 1981.

Tugendhat, Ernst. *Ti Kata Tinos.* Freiburg i. Br.: Karl Alber Verlag, 1958.

Whitehead, Alfred North. *Adventures of Ideas.* New York: Macmillan, 1933.

———. *Process and Reality: An Essay in Cosmology.* Corrected Edition edited by David Ray Griffin and Donald W. Sherburne. New York: The Free Press, 1978.

———. *Science and the Modern World.* 18th printing. New York: Macmillan, 1967.

Wieland, Wolfgang. *Schellings Lehre von der Zeit.* Heidelberg: Winter Verlag, 1956.

Articles

Bracken, Joseph A. "Authentic Subjectivity and Genuine Objectivity." *Horizons* 11 (1984): 290–303.

———. "Subsistent Relation: Mediating Concept for a New Synthesis?" *Journal of Religion* 64 (1984): 188–204.

Braeckman, Antoon. "Whitehead and German Idealism: A Poetic Heritage." *Process Studies* 14 (1984–85): 265–86.

Cobb, John B., Jr. "Overcoming Reductionism." In *Existence and Actuality: Conversations with Charles Hartshorne.* Edited by John Cobb and Franklin Gamwell. Chicago: University of Chicago Press, 1984.

———. "Response to Loomer." In *The Size of God: The Theology of Bernard Loomer in Context.* Edited by William Dean and Larry E. Axel. Macon, Ga: Mercer University Press, 1987.

Earley, Joseph E. "Self-Organization and Agency: In Chemistry and in Process Philosophy." *Process Studies* 11 (1981): 242–58.

Frankenberry, Nancy. "The Power of the Past." *Process Studies* 13 (1983): 132–42.

Fredericks, James, S. S. "The Kyoto School: Modern Buddhist Philosophy and the Search for a Transcultural Theology." *Horizons* 15 (1988): 299–315.

Garland, William J. "Whitehead's Theory of Causal Objectification." *Process Studies* 12 (1982): 180–91.

Griffin, David Ray. "Bohm and Whitehead on Wholeness, Freedom, Causality and Time." In *Physics and the Ultimate Significance of Time.* Albany: State University of New York Press, 1986.

———. "The Possibility of Subjective Immortality in Whitehead's Philosophy." *Modern Schoolman* 53 (1975–76): 39–57.

Hartshorne, Charles. "The Compound Individual." In *Philosophical Essays for Alfred North Whitehead*. Edited by F. S. C. Northrup. New York: Russell and Russell, 1936.

King, J. Norman, and Barry L. Whitney. "Rahner and Hartshorne on Death and Eternal Life." *Horizons* 15 (1988): 239–61.

Lee, Bernard J. "Loomer on Deity: A Long Night's Journey into Day." In *The Size of God: The Theology of Bernard Loomer in Context*. Edited by William Dean and Larry E. Axel. Macon, Ga: Mercer University Press, 1987.

Lindsay, James E., Jr. "The Misapprehension of Presentational Immediacy." *Process Studies* 14 (1985): 145–57.

Loomer, Bernard M. "The Size of God." In *The Size of God: The Theology of Bernard Loomer in Context*. Edited by William Dean and Larry E. Axel. Macon, Ga: Mercer University Press, 1987.

Lucas, George R., Jr. "Evolutionist Theories and Whitehead's Philosophy." *Process Studies* 14 (1984–85): 287–300.

Pannenberg, Wolfhart. "Atom, Duration, Form: Difficulties with Process Philosophy." *Process Studies* 14 (1984–85): 21–30.

Shimony, Abner. "Quantum Physics and the Philosophy of Whitehead." In *Boston Studies in the Philosophy of Science*. Vol. 2. Edited by Robert S. Cohen and Marx W. Wartofsky. New York: Humanities Press, 1965.

Stapp, Henry. "Einstein Time and Process Time." In *Physics and the Ultimate Significance of Time*. Albany: State University of New York Press, 1986.

———. "Mind, Matter, and Quantum Mechanics," *Foundations of Physics* 12 (1982): 381–83.

Vater, Michael. "Heidegger and Schelling: The Finitude of Being." *Idealistic Studies* 5 (1975): 20–58.

Zeltner, Hermann. "Gleichgewicht als Seinsprinzip, Schellings Philosophie des Gleichgewichts." *Studium Generale* 14 (1961): 498–504.

Index

Abgrund, 97, 174 n.19

Absolute Emptiness, 163–64, 181 n.10

Absolute Spirit, 106, 108

Actual occasion, 97, 105, 119, 134, 141, 162, 164, 171 n.12, 175 nn. 41, 45, and 46, 178 nn. 16 and 18, 179 nn. 2 and 6, 180 n.33; within the cosmic society, 147–52, 157–58; and Creativity, 128, 132; and the divine persons, 124, 126; objective and subjective immortality of, 135–39, 142–47; and quantum physics, 62–63; and probability distribution, 64–66; and societies, 42–49, 109–12; and structured societies, 67–72, 80–86, 129–30; and temporal consciousness, 102–4. *See also* Agency of actual occasions; Self-constitution of actual occasions; Society, unity of Whiteheadian

Adventures of Ideas, 42, 45, 47, 114, 115–16, 118, 158–59, 169 n.13, 171 n.5

Agency of actual occasions: collective agency of actual occasions, 14, 43–44, 45–49, 51–56, 112–14, 117–18, 119; individual agencies of actual occasions, 14, 43–44, 45–49, 51–52, 55–56, 117–18, 119

Aggregates, as opposed to ontological totalities, 40–42, 44, 48, 49, 53, 66, 70, 106, 107, 109–12

Ambiguity of the reality of God, 156–58

Aquinas, Thomas, 24–26, 151, 177 n.4

Aristotle, 23–25, 40–41, 52–55, 92, 95, 111, 166 nn. 10 and 12, 169 n.7, 177 n.4

Atomism (metaphysical), 40, 48

Barbour, Ian, 33, 57

Becoming, metaphysics of, 22, 33–34, 153–54

Being, reality of, 21–35, 41, 48, 91, 152, 181 n.10; ontological difference between Being and beings, 94–95, 99–100. *See also* God; Nature; Process (cosmic)

Bodies, 40–42, 69, 72, 108. *See also* Material elements

Bracken, Joseph, 96, 174 n.19

Braeckman, Antoon, 174 n.12, 175 n.34

Buber, Martin, 101

Buddhism, 140, 163–64

Causal efficacy, 41–42, 157

Causality, 24–25, 30, 41–42, 166 n.12, 169 n.12, 175 n.46; as process of grounding, 92–97. *See also* Ground-Consequent relation

Christian, William, 180 n.33

Clausius, Rudolph, 74

Cobb, John, 17, 42–43, 45, 47, 48, 55–56, 155, 169 nn. 15 and 17, 179 n.2

Code, Murray, 67, 172 nn. 23 and 28

Collins, James, 105

Common element of form, 44–45, 46, 51, 54–55, 60, 86, 105, 109, 111, 112, 119, 128; as probability distribution, 64–66; within structured societies, 70–72, 80–84

Community, 15, 39, 48, 50, 55, 60, 65, 68, 69–70, 87, 162, 172 n.33; as civil society or state, 114–18, 119, 176 n.20; divine community, 124–29, 132, 133–34, 138. *See also* Cosmic society

Compound individuals, 43, 49

Concept (Hegelian), 28–29, 106–9, 111, 118

Concrescence of actual occasion, 100,